Praise from the Reviewers

"This book is unique in the recent North American literature on bilingual/multicultural education and addresses an important and often neglected area: the affective dimensions of immigrant childrens' experience and the relationship of this experience to academic development. . . .

A strong message from the book is that, at some level, all teachers of immigrant/culturally diverse students must become researchers if they are to teach effectively since no theory can supply the answers to the range of issues teachers are faced with in our increasingly diverse schools. . . .

The voice and struggles of the author are expressed eloquently and speak directly to the many thousands of teachers who are struggling to adjust to a radically new demographic reality. For mainstream teachers who are looking for ideas and inspiration the book has some very important messages. It also links up with theory in powerful ways. . . . This book will be greatly appreciated by teachers who will see their own struggles mirrored in the author's reflections and observations."

—Jim Cummins, *The Ontario Institute for Studies in Education*

"This is the most truthful, informative, relevant, and powerful book I have read in a while . . . and I must say, I have read some powerful ones. . . . Cristina Igoa makes you respond to her words! She engages you in the discourse and you cannot help but to "talk to her." . . . This book is in the forefront of an educational agenda that critically transforms what is practiced in schools today. . . . It is a must for all teachers—in training, in the field, supervising, mentoring. . . . It is one of a kind. . . . If you are to ask me what I see as the best feature of this text . . . I would have to say it is *Cristina Igoa*. A teacher engaged in a never-ending dialogue with her students and thus herself. . . . Thank you for this wonderful reading experience."

—Irma J. O'Neill,
State University of New York, College at Old Westbury

"I think this is a terrific book. It is highly readable, engaging, and free of educational jargon.... It demonstrates the enormously positive role that one teacher can have. I kept thinking as I was reading how lucky her students were, and how I would want *all* immigrant children to have Cristina Igoa as their teacher....

This is a wonderful book and I believe it will join the ranks of other inspiring accounts that can motivate and energize teachers who work with immigrant students."
—Sonia Nieto, *The University of Massachusetts, Amherst*

"This timely book tells an inspiring story of immigrant children through the eyes and experience of a gifted and dedicated teacher, herself from an immigrant background. All that she advocates pedagogically she has modelled in her own teaching career....

I value the first-person storytelling mode of this eminently readable book and the absence of jargon. At the same time it is clear that the author is fully cognizant of current educational theory and confident enough to modify that theory when her experience contradicts it.

I especially value how much this teacher allows herself to learn from her students and their families. Educators pay lip service to this concept; very few of us really build this attitude into our pedagogy. I also value the many ways that the author employs the arts as "language" to give voice to the experience of the immigrant child.

There is much more than inspiration here. For the teacher in today's multicultural classroom, this book offers much valuable information about the psychology of the immigrant child, about bridging the cultural gaps with families, and about useful pedagogical tools."
—Sister Margaret Hoffman, S.N.D., former chairperson,
dept. of art, *College of Notre Dame,* Belmont (CA)

The Inner World
of the
Immigrant Child

The
Inner World
of the
Immigrant Child

CRISTINA IGOA

Hayward (CA) Unified School District
and College of Notre Dame, Belmont (CA)

 LAWRENCE ERLBAUM ASSOCIATES, PUBLISHERS
Mahwah, New Jersey

Dedicated to all immigrant children—may their voices
be heard by teachers and administrators so that they
reach their fullest potential and feel truly alive in school

Lawrence Erlbaum Associates, Inc., Publishers
10 Industrial Avenue
Mahwah, New Jersey 07430

ISBN 0-8058-8013-5

Library of Congress Catalog Card Number 94-65156

Books published by Lawrence Erlbaum Associates are printed
on acid-free paper, and their bindings are chosen
for strength and durability.

Printed in the United States of America

10 9

Photo Credits

Page 124 *left* courtesy Kamila Kepa; page 124 *right* courtesy Mejghan Nizam; pages
130 and 170, courtesy Jim Chan; pages 141 and 171 courtesy Cristina Igoa. *Photo
Montage:* Photographs at top right and bottom right (*left page*) and top left and
center left (*right page*) courtesy Jim Chan; other photographs courtesy Cristina Igoa.

Foreword

Native Americans, the descendants of those original inhabitants of this country who were able to survive centuries of invasion and genocide, are the only people who can rightfully claim that they are neither the product of immigration nor of forcible abduction to the United States. Yet, while attitudes toward our immigrant ancestors range from nostalgia to benign indifference, the attitude toward present-day immigrants, at every point in history, has been predominantly one of fear and contempt. It is as though this country would like to take pride in the symbol of the Statue of Liberty, yet decree that its welcoming stance applies only to the historical past.

In spite of these attitudes, immigrants continue to arrive, not only flying in on airplaines and passing through customs offices, but also being washed to our shores or hidden in truck beds, still wet from crossing the river. Still others overextend their visitor's stay. Adults make the difficult and often even risky decision to immigrate because they are escaping from war and famine, fleeing from political persecution, or inspired by desires for better living standards. For those that are parents, or plan to be parents, the greatest hope is that their children will have a better future, and they trust that children's resilience and flexibility will keep them from suffering too greatly as the result of the uprooting. There seems to be, after all, a generalized assumption that children can adapt easily. The paucity of literature on the difficulties experienced by immigrant children and the lack of counseling services specifically designed to deal with the traumas of immigration suggest that the general public is either not aware or has little concern for the difficulties of the transition immigrant families experience.

Educators working with immigrant children know better. They see their silence, their reluctance, their shyness. They know there is far more than meets the eye in their struggle to do well in school or in their giving up on the process.

More and more bilingual and ESL teachers, like Cristina Igoa, have begun to ask immigrant children to tell their stories, and to invite their parents to share their stories as well. The work in California of Valerie Balderas in the Salinas-Watsonville area, of Nancy Jean Smith in Stockton, of Barbara Moreno in Los Angeles, of Sylvia Dorta-Duque de Reyes in San Diego, and of Sudia Paloma McCaleb in San Francisco, and the work in Puerto Rico and throughout the United States of Kristin Brown (Project ORILLAS) are excellent examples of this approach. As children examine the painful decisions their parents had to make, as they recognize that it will not be easy for their family hopes to come true, as they face the difficulties that adaptation entails, they begin to heal the wounds of separation and to accept the demanding task of creating a new worldview that includes the heritage they bring and the reality they encounter in their new country. These teachers are reaching beyond just the techniques of whole language into the areas of critical pedagogy or transformative education, which recognize human beings' capacity to construct knowledge, and in the process of doing so, begin to transform reality.

Cristina Igoa brings her unique personal focus to this work by providing children the opportunity to reveal themselves in the safety of the nest she creates for them in her classroom. Through this process she is able to gather extraordinary material, to look beyond the story line into the depths of the souls of immigrant children. With great sensitivity and insight, she uncovers the symbols in her students' narratives. But rather than appropriating the meaning by imposing her own interpretation on the material, she has, true to the spirit of participatory research, chosen to return to the children a few years later and invited them to analyze their own experience through dialogic retrospection.

What she has learned from these students, as a result of their dialogue together, she shares with us in the first part of this unusual book. The students reveal for the reader the richness and complexity of that silent period in which children are confronted with giving up all they know and accepting that their lives have changed completely. But Cristina is not satisfied just to arrive at new knowledge. She proceeds to utilize what she has learned from the students to reflect further upon her own practice and uses that reflection to take the next steps in her evolution as a teacher by engaging her new students in the process of actively reflecting on their experiences as immigrants as they are living them. This she shares with us in the second part of the book.

"To learn to read is to learn to walk. To learn to write is to learn to rise." In this lapidary statement, José Martí, one of the greatest educators of this hemisphere, reminds us that while reading opens the mind and spirit to the possibilities of knowledge and allows us to walk the path of understanding, it is through writing that we discover our voice and by speaking our truth that we begin to shape a new reality.

Cristina Igoa, with profound intuition, understood that uprooted immigrant children would not be able to truly benefit from a dialogue with their new reality until they had the opportunity to express the intricacy of their inner world. She did not allow the children's incipient abilities with the English language to limit them: she found a medium for their expression by encouraging them first to draw the stories they wanted to tell. The fact that the children chose to represent themselves symbolically, by means of animals and objects, in order to protect their own vulnerability, in no way obscures the fact that they were writing about themselves. When the final products, the filmstrips developed by the children, were completed, the children had become both authors and protagonists.

"*To be a teacher is to be a creator,*" affirms José Martí. And Cristina Igoa has known how to be a teacher, a true creator, in her innovative use of classroom space, of instructional time, and of the means she has developed to facilitate the expression of her students.

It is a great joy to participate, with this foreword, in the completion of this long and illuminating journey. As this book so clearly shows, dissertations need not be a dry academic exercise in pursuit of a degree, but can and ought to be a vibrant experience in reflection that enriches the wider community.

As I celebrate Naomi Silverman's vision in welcoming the manuscript of this book and shepherding it to its final form, I also wish to thank the Office of Bilingual Education and Language Minorities (Title VII of the Department of Education) for granting Cristina Igoa a Doctoral Fellowship at the University of San Francisco, during which I had the privilege to work with her and to see this book begin to take form. Our immigrant students deserve support at all levels, from early grades on through advanced degrees, if indeed they are to share their talents and the depths of their inner vision with everyone and thus enrich everyone's world.

Alma Flor Ada
University of San Francisco

Preface

What goes on in the inner world of the immigrant child?
Would it help the child if the teacher knew? Would the
teacher's approach and methodologies be different? Or would
the teacher use the same ones, but with a different purpose?

When immigrant children leave the country that was their home—a familiar language, culture, community, and social system—they experience a variety of emotional and cognitive adjustments to the reality of life in a new country. How dry and clinical that sentence sounds! It doesn't even begin to convey the paralyzing fear in a little boy from Afghanistan that he will never fully understand English, that he will always be on the outside, looking in. It doesn't explain why an achievement-oriented girl from Vietnam will intentionally fail tests that might advance her in the educational system. And it certainly doesn't tell all you need to know about the intense loneliness of a little girl from South America who, caught between two cultures and moved from class to class, school to school, cannot communicate easily in any language. As a teacher of immigrant children myself, I have worked with children like these for many years.

The Inner World of the Immigrant Child is about experience. It is not about the larger economic, social, and historical circumstances of immigration—although, of course, these are important and cannot be ignored. It is not about empirical "scientific" research on child development, learning theories, and teaching methods. It is, in essence, an account of qualitative research that reveals what goes on in the hearts and minds of immigrant children.

This text shares one teacher's world—my own. It is written in narrative form so the reader can understand not only the development of the immigrant child but also the development of a teacher who tries to honor, in her daily work with the children, each one's unique inner world.

Unlike more general texts on bilingual, ESL (English as a Second Language), and multicultural education, this book focuses specifically on immigrant children—a large and growing segment of students in today's schools. The book treats them not as invisible members of the population of all culturally diverse "language minority" students (who are typically lumped together in school) but as children who share the particular experience of being uprooted and finding themselves in a new and unfamiliar country.

My own story—as both a teacher of immigrant children and an immigrant myself—is intertwined with the voices and artwork of children with whom I have worked. Part I portrays the immigrant experience of uprooting, culture shock, and adjustment to a new world. Part II describes a threefold theoretical model of cultural/academic/psychological (CAP) interventions for working with immigrant children that facilitates learning as they make the transition to a new language and culture. The model I present has evolved from my own work with these students as well as my research and scholarship over the years.

Central to my work, and to this book, is an emphasis on listening to the children as the first step. I do not offer a "formula" to be replicated mechanically; rather, by telling my story, I hope to engage readers in a process of observation, reflection, and inquiry that can serve as a starting point for developing understanding and teaching practices that are relevant to their own current or future classroom situations.

As the book unfolds:

I outline and explain step-by-step how I developed my present teaching methodology, based on my philosophy of educating children. I share my struggles in the classroom and with the school system, the insights I gained as I listened to my students in an effort to understand their needs and feelings and as I worked with them to develop responsibility for their own educational progress and to facilitate their successful transition into the "mainstream" curriculum.

I explain my view of why and how literacy is central to learning and to the child's sense of self-empowerment, and I detail specific classroom practices that contribute to building literacy while also motivating children to become active learners.

I describe program designs that are meant to work alongside already existing educational programs in the schools. These programs are meant to serve as examples, which can be adapted to particular situations, for restructuring classrooms in ways that personalize teaching and move it away from the "factory model" of education.

In the last pages of this book I have provided a bibliography that includes the work of other authors who have contributed to the field and whose work and thinking are stimulating and inspiring.

The Inner World of the Immigrant Child is intended for all interested readers concerned with the education of immigrant children in today's schools. It is written, however, specifically as a text for pre-service and in-service teachers, to be read in a range of courses on teaching culturally diverse children, multicultural education, English as a Second Language, and literacy education. It is also appropriate for any social foundations of education course or content-area methods course (especially elementary reading and language arts methods) that integrates attention to or includes a component on cultural diversity and/or second language learners and for courses on participatory research and teachers as researchers.

Join me now as I tell my story. Listen to the voices of the immigrant children in our schools. My hope is that you may find these stories helpful in understanding the needs and feelings of immigrant children and in finding your own ways to facilitate their transition between two worlds.

Acknowledgments

I express my deepest gratitude to Naomi Silverman, my editor, whose dedicated energy, encouragement, vision, and confidence in the work has inspired me to write. It is her commitment to the children and the time she devoted to the editorial work that has made this book possible. I am grateful for the friendship that has evolved through the years in dialogue with her.

I thank the St. Martin's Press reviewers and editors whose detailed comments and criticisms expanded and challenged my thinking for greater clarity and cohesiveness. To these reviewers and editors, I am grateful: Jim Cummins, Ontario Institute for Studies in Education; Bernardo Gallegos, California State University–Los Angeles; Sonia Nieto, University of Massachusetts; Irma J. O'Neill, State University of New York at Old Westbury; Carolyn Panofsky, Rhode Island College; Patricia Ramsey, Mount Holyoke College; and Henry T. Trueba, University of Wisconsin–Madison. I also appreciate the efforts of project editor Diana Puglisi, who coordinated the production of the manuscript.

I am indebted to Dr. Brian Gerard, Dr. and Mrs. George Wilson, and Florence Grossenbacher, M.A. Their theoretical guidance challenged my thinking and encouraged me to delve deeper into the research and work with immigrant children.

Many colleagues and scholars gave generously of their time, intellectual support, and ideas. I thank Dr. Tove Skutnabb-Kangas, Margaret Mary Hoffman, S.N.D., Dr. Thomas Hart, Dr. Rosemary Dalton, Dr. Diane Guay, Dr. Joel Spring, Dr. Judith Barker, Sandra Rogers-Hare, Dr. Aida Joshi, and Dr. Mark Sullivan.

The children and I have been enriched by Dr. Constance Beutel and the Self-Directed Education team at Pacific Bell. To those who spoke with and visited the children, listened to their reading, and searched for books and materials for the classroom, I am grateful.

I thank my family members Jose, Bettina, and Isabel, along with my extended family, for their support and enthusiasm. My niece Deborah is appreciated for the time she devoted to visiting and corresponding with the children. The encouraging words of my nieces and nephews are likewise appreciated.

My special thanks are due to my father Rafael and my brother Rafael, as well as to Tom McCall; they gave much of their valuable time, reading my text and providing insightful suggestions.

Thanks, too, to my aunt, Celeste C. Calvo, for her patience, efficiency, meticulous typing, retyping, editing, and checking of references. For her generosity of time and work, I am most indebted.

I would like to recognize Janet Simons's intellectual support and assistance with the organization of the last chapters and for the diagram of the "Closing of the Gaps." My thanks are also due to Jim Chan of Photo 28 in Haywood, California, for photographs and for film processing of the photos submitted to my publisher.

Also, many thanks to Gynne Stern for endless hours of stimulating thinking and for the insights I gained in my conversations with her.

To Rahima Asefi Haya for her untiring efforts and support in the classroom and her assistance in connecting me with the children of Afghanistan and their parents; and to Mary Martinez and Yen Diep for their assistance in working with these children, I am thankful.

I thank my friends at Redeemer Church of San Rafael, California: Rev. Jack Schanhaar for his interest, feedback, and suggestions, and Molly Taylor and George and Gail Wilson for the clothing contributions for the refugee children and for their interest in the work.

To my friends who encouraged me, read, and applauded *The Inner World of the Immigrant Child* through to the finish, I am grateful: Antoinette Ortenzo, Guillermo Ayesa, Gloria Rognoni, Terry Kreutzmann, Sr. Mercedes, O.C.D., Bernadette Barnes, Monica May, Hugo and Linda Reynolds, Beverly Spencer, Maria Villani, Paulette Sylvester, and Francisco Ortenzo.

I am grateful to Dr. Alma Flor Ada of the University of San Francisco, who challenged my thinking and from whom I have learned a great deal. I am honored to have her voice in the foreword.

A special word of acknowledgment to all the students I have been privileged to teach and to those who gave of themselves and voiced their thoughts to make this book happen.

Cristina Igoa

Contents

2 The Phenomenon of Uprooting   37

3 Entering the Inner World of the Immigrant Child   70

PART TWO

Teaching Immigrant Students: Integrating the Cultural/Academic/Psychological Dimensions of the Whole Child   111

4 Cultural/Academic/Psychological Interventions   113

Prologue

Teaching, I believe, is an art. Between the ideal and the real, teachers struggle to improve as each year passes. I make every effort to create a positive environment for learning and ask my students to do the same.

Rapport with students is very important, and the teacher attempts to build this within the first few months of the year. I listen attentively to what students have to say, because regardless of age they are individuals who have a lot to express and whose thoughts need to be heard. I do all I can to give them the freedom to be honest with me, as I am with them.

Because I respect them, I include students' ideas whenever possible in the lesson plan and ask them to take as much responsibility for learning as they can. It is their education, so they need to be involved in it.

I see myself as a guide—one who walks with students through the content I am entrusted to teach. Teaching in a cheerful and friendly manner brings that same spirit out of them. I bring up subjects that will evoke the curiosity that has been present in children since they were born. While stretching their minds to develop analytical skills, I try not to discount the importance of feelings—for I believe it is vital to educate the whole person, not just a part of the person. I work at taking the tediousness out of the humdrum and bringing out the creative in my students, and I take time to look for methods to lead them to seek knowledge.

1

Like the artist who experiments on canvas to find the best colors, to brush and to blend, the teacher paints on the canvas of the classroom, interacting, learning, growing. I am involved in the art of working with and calling for the best in all my students.

Introduction

I love my country very much. I will never forget it wherever I am.

GIRL FROM AFGHANISTAN, AGE 11½

Immigrant children have individual histories and inner struggles as they wrestle with the changes in their lives. Their development began in another country; their lives were first attuned to a different culture. Even after they have been in the United States for some time, when they are asked to express their thoughts about the country of their birth, it is evident that they still feel connected to their homeland.

Our challenge as teachers is to know how to reach these children, to teach them, to know what to do when they reveal—or cannot express—themselves to us. But with every challenge successfully undertaken, I believe we contribute to the world. Teaching, then, becomes purposeful.

I became interested in understanding the immigrant child's world over fifteen years ago, when I began to design a classroom for twenty immigrant children. This classroom later became known as the "Center." Here I worked closely with the children to develop their literacy skills in English and to develop their writing ability, using art and storytelling as motivating factors for them to learn to read and write.

3

It was at the Center that I met Dennis and the other children you will encounter in this book, who illustrated their imaginative stories by making filmstrips. During their time at the Center some of these children were silent, unable or unwilling to communicate in English. My task was to work with that silence. I began then to reflect on my own experience as an immigrant child and used part of those reflections as a resource for working with the children. For two years we worked together, and the compelling stories produced by the children conveyed intriguing messages that I attempted to interpret as the children slowly, very carefully, began to reveal themselves to me.

Later, as part of my doctoral dissertation at the University of San Francisco, I reacquainted myself with some of my former students, who were now on the verge of adulthood. It was very important for me to both confirm my initial interpretations and view the filmstrips with these former students to awaken their recollections and discover their interpretation. School counselors at the local high schools assisted me in locating the students. Five enthusiastic young people, all from Southeast Asian countries, volunteered to make themselves available to delve deeper into their immigrant experience and to share their inner worlds. Two others, one from Mexico and one from Samoa, also volunteered and entered into the experience; but they returned to their homelands before the research was complete. This is not the place to explore the reasons why all five young people who agreed to talk with me about their earlier filmstrips were—coincidentally or not—immigrants from Southeast Asia. The important point is that the themes that emerged from our dialogues and from the images in the filmstrips made by other children (from Samoa,[1] Mexico, the Philippines, and El Salvador) cut across all cultures. The children all had in common the phenomenon of uprooting and the emotions that emerge from such an experience, and some shared the experience of the silent stage at school.

Having completed my doctorate, and armed with the knowledge gained from working at the Center and my later dialogues with the children, I went back into the public schools and immersed myself in a Sheltered English classroom of 5th and 6th grade immigrant children. Children in this Sheltered English classroom did not compete academically with native English speakers, whose English fluency is assumed. There were as many as eight different languages spoken in

[1] American Samoa is a territory of the United States and Western Samoa is an independent country. The inhabitants of American Samoa are nationals, but not American citizens (Schramm et al., 1981). Although they may emigrate to the United States without passports, the children who come to the United States mainland experience the uprooting inwardly in the same way as immigrant children from other countries. Therefore, children from American Samoa (as well as children from Guam) are discussed in this book.

the classroom. Here the children and I were on common ground. Because I myself had come to the United States as an immigrant child, we all understood what it meant to have been uprooted and transplanted. We were aware of cultural differences, the loss of signs of the familiar, and the fragmented education experienced by many because of travel and relocation. Some of us had traveled through other countries and, in many cases, shared a war experience.

Connections: My Own Experience as a Newcomer and My Quest to Understand the Immigrant Child

Immigrant Children and the Experience of War

While working with the children from war-torn countries, I recalled my own experience of dislocation from one country to another during wartime and empathized as they spoke or wrote about the horrors of war. I was born in the Philippines and was 5 years old when my family left the islands two months before the end of World War II. Manila was still occupied by the Japanese when our entire family boarded a U.S. Army transport for the United States. Aboard ship, wartime regulations were in force. All the women and small children were confined to one side of the ship, the men to the other. We had constant drills on what to do in case of submarine or air attack. We were told not to throw pieces of paper over the side of the ship because the enemy might track our progress by seeing bits of paper floating on the water.

When we arrived in Los Angeles, my father's job search offered him several options. He finally took a position in Central America. I was still 5 when we moved to Central America and then to Colombia, South America, where I started school. I convinced my parents that school was too painful and that home was a safer place, so they allowed me to leave school and study at home. Three years later my family returned to the Philippines.

When, at age 13, I again traveled across the Pacific because my family was returning to the United States, my leave-taking was less frightening; it was peacetime and there was no fear of enemy attack. But once again I had to accustom myself to a new school and a new culture.

Similarly, many immigrant children I work with have not only experienced war but have had to accustom themselves to a new school and a new culture. Nurturance is what they need, but not the kind of nurturance that weakens them or fosters dependence on the teacher, thereby perpetuating childish and dependent behavior rather than allowing the children to grow and become self-reliant.

Three recollections from my early school years surfaced when I began teaching immigrant children. The first was the importance of having a best friend—in my case, a Chinese girl who was schooled with me and moved along with me from class to class. The second was that moving from class to class detracted from the learning process. I had forgotten these experiences until two children whom you will meet later in this book, Rosario and Dung, reminded me of their own similar experiences. The third recollection was that I had become fascinated by myths and fairy tales. In those stories I could find courage through reading about heroes and heroines and the slaying of dragons. I used the memory of this experience when I worked with Dennis, whom you will meet in Chapter 1.

Fragmented Formal Schooling

My formal schooling during childhood was fragmented, as schooling has been for most immigrant children. I spent a few months in kindergarten in South America. After we returned to the Philippines I was 8 years old and started first grade. Although I spoke Spanish, I attended a school where all grades were taught in English. My second grade year was incomplete, as teachers temporarily placed me in an age-appropriate grade level (third grade) and then back in second grade again. Soon a change in our residence meant I had to attend another school, where I was placed in the fourth grade because of my age. When we returned to the United States I was placed in the eighth grade, again because of my age. Thus I skipped both the third and seventh grades. Living in three countries, however, I did receive an expansive and informal "global" education during my formative years.

Although I sensed the gaps in my formal education as I grew older and went through the school system, I was not able to close the gaps until I began teaching. As I moved from teaching first grade to teaching upper-level grades, I mastered the teaching of each grade level and became familiar with the developmental stages of children in each grade.

More than 75 percent of the more than 100 immigrant children I have worked with in the past fifteen years have experienced gaps in their education because of travel, time needed for preparation of exit and entry documents, and moving around in search of a better home. Many children have skipped one grade or more.

My family is from Poland. I was ten years old when I came to Amerika. Before I came, we stopped at another country. I don't remember the name of it. . . .

First they placed me in second grade. In second grade I was one week. Then I went to fourth grade. In fourth grade I was five months. Then I went to fifth grade. In fifth grade I was five months also. Now I am in the sixth grade.

GIRL FROM POLAND, AGE 12

Some children who had come from war-torn countries were un-schooled or partially schooled or had been schooled at refugee camps. Some children had been left in their homeland temporarily with their mothers and siblings or other relatives while the fathers went ahead to the United States to find a place to live. Some of the older ones had to stay out of school to help their mothers.

Inquiry and Reflection: My Experience as a Teacher–Researcher

I spoke with these children and began to design a curriculum for them. Their individual stories were documented in filmstrips, tapes, videotapes, journals, drawings, compositions, and reports. As I gathered the children's creations, they taught me how to read them. I was able to use their work to help them respond favorably to school; their work provided a way to bridge their former world and their present one. Following a rigorous academic plan I prepared, they were able to bridge the gaps in their education as well. I realized that there really is no formula, that the most effective approach was to become a teacher–researcher. In this role I had to find out first who my students were, where they were from, how much education they had experienced, and how I could move them forward.

So with every group of students who enter my classroom each year, I start all over and we "paint" a new picture, "write" a new story—our class picture and story—as together we interact, learn, and grow.

Action: A Threefold Model of Cultural/Academic/Psychological Interventions

Many teachers have asked where and how I begin. This book outlines and explains step by step how I came to my present philosophy—the threefold cultural/academic/psychological (CAP) intervention that began to evolve after my encounter with Dennis. The goals of the CAP intervention are to facilitate the child's maintenance of authenticity and connection to his or her native culture, academic achievement, and sense of feeling fully alive in school. This approach gives rise to a supportive and cooperative environment for both students and teachers. The book tells the story of two completely different school settings: the Center and a Sheltered English classroom.

Differentiation between Empowerment and Power

In the first experience with immigrant children (the Center), I was given an ideal situation both academically and financially to set up a classroom specifically for the children. I felt empowered. It is important to differentiate between (1) the meaning of empowerment as I am using it here, and (2) the meaning of power that is invested in an individual or in an institution and can be used to impose values, expectations, or goals on individuals or groups that they themselves do not generate or recognize. In the latter, the person or persons *use* power to control others; they are "caught in power." Empowerment means something else entirely. Nobody can empower another person—people can only empower (give power to) themselves; this becomes possible when they have an internalized sense of self-confidence that generates purposeful action on their own behalf.

The distinction is relevant here because in the second school setting, I had to work within the constraints found in most school systems. Although I never lost my own sense of empowerment, I found that the power invested in the institution of the school sometimes stood in the way of my doing what I felt was most effective for the children. In this case, my struggles in the classroom and with the school system may have hindered some expression of my fullest potential to work with the children in my class, as doors were shut before me to give credence to the "status quo"; but it also challenged my initiative to find other doors to slip through—even a window, if I had to. The important point is that I never lost faith that school failure is seldom, if ever, the child's fault. When one engages in a thorough investigation of the child's environment, intellectual or emotional failures often are found to be a result of undercurrents between the child and adult and/or the institution wherein the child feels unloved (Wickes, 1988), unchallenged, and disempowered.

What Can a Teacher Do?

Those of us who work with children know that our task is complicated; we have to examine the teaching practices we use, the policies we are expected to follow, the theories we adopt. In the end, regardless of policies, philosophies, theories, and methodologies, the success or failure of an individual child—the way that child experiences school—depends on what happens in that child's classroom, what kind of learning environment the teacher is able to provide, and how well the teacher is able to investigate and attend to the particular needs of that child.

Immigrant children are more than "language minority" children. They are children who have been uprooted from their own cultural environment and who need to be guided not to fling themselves overboard in their encounter with a new culture—for some, a "powerful" culture—and with a new language. As teachers, we need to help them open up to the new while they retain the old. We need to help them learn to succeed so they can be productive and contribute to worldwide civilization.

The program design presented in this book can work alongside already existing educational programs in the schools, and it can be refined to meet the needs of particular situations. Throughout the pages of this book, the underlying message is that the school system needs to change. A teacher cannot do it all.

Rigid school policies can create disempowering environments such as the one I experienced as I worked with the children in the second school system. Here I voiced my objections to the rigidity and inequalities in the system. Whenever the occasion warranted or the children themselves complained of oppression or discrimination in the schoolyard and misunderstandings with teachers and administrators, I showed them how to stand up for themselves, how to voice their thoughts intelligently and in a manner that could be heard. Sometimes they were heard, sometimes not. But try, we did.

The underlying message is also that classrooms need to change so that teachers can become more than dispensers of information. We need to humanize our classrooms to best teach our students and facilitate the development of literacy, which is the most self-empowering skill a child can gain in school.

On the whole, I have found that most immigrant parents want their children to have a good education. For this, they struggle to survive and find jobs to support their family in the new country. They want their children to succeed in school, to belong to the new society, and to make new friends without losing their cultural values.

There is much a teacher can do to awaken the power within the children to help themselves and to feel empowered. When I am exhausted, I know they are leaning on me too much. When I direct the energy back on them and expect them to succeed, the children respond, develop, and are alive; and I am refreshed. The children and the teacher are in a creative mode.

Throughout the past fifteen years of teaching immigrant children, I have been asked if my work is not meant for all children. The answer is yes, all children can benefit from this approach. But I needed to focus first on the phenomenon of the immigration of children, to observe what happens when a child is uprooted from his or her homeland and has to start again in a new school, a new culture, a new language. What takes place in the mind of the child when the phenomenon of uprooting happens? How does the child respond to school? I wanted (1) to observe the immediacy of the experience as it relates to children immigrating into the United States currently, and (2) to see not only what happens to the children in the schools during the immigration process but also its consequences for their development.

What I have learned can be applied to all children in the public schools in one way or another. I have seen many U.S.-born children in cultural conflict with each other. I have seen children restless, fragmented, and in cultural conflict with themselves. For them, integration of their inner and outer selves, a sense of being at home with themselves and in the world, may be a more difficult task—but it is not impossible. Clearly, many aspects of the threefold intervention, cultural/academic/psychological, can be applied. A few points are clear:

The importance of listening to the children
The importance of the feeling of having roots
The importance of understanding cultures
The importance of belonging

This book begins with the story of an immigrant boy from Mao Tse-Tung's China who hid himself from the world to which he wished to belong.

PART ONE

Understanding the Needs and Feelings of Immigrant Children

1

The Silent Stage

This is a totally different environment than I have been used to. The change is different because it upsets the kind of life I had. It was different back home. School was different, teachers were different. I feel depressed because I miss my friends in my country.

IMMIGRANT CHILD FROM CHINA, AGE 11

Dennis

Dennis stood by my classroom door. He was a small, serious, visibly frightened 12-year-old boy. I asked him to come in and sit at the table I had prepared. I had been told by his previous teacher that there was a "problem." Dennis had spent the past school year without speaking to anyone. In the schoolyard he always sat on a bench in silence. A year is an eternity for a child to be locked up inside, I thought.

Dennis was clearly Chinese, but his name, Dennis, confused me— it didn't fit him. I knew he had come from the Hunan Province of Mainland China, which had been under the domination of Chairman Mao for many years. Both his parents had been doctors in China, but now his father carried crates in San Francisco's Chinatown for a living. The other Asian students in the school were from Hong Kong and Vietnam, and Dennis didn't connect with these children.

Gently, I gave Dennis a paper and pencil and gestured to him to write his name in Chinese. If I could help him feel at home, I thought, and show him that I appreciated and valued who he was as a person, including his Chineseness, perhaps he would relax and allow me to teach him. Picking up the pencil obediently, Dennis began to form some lines, but abruptly he pushed the pencil away and shook his head with an emphatic "No!" At that moment, he revealed to me the energy and force inside him. He acted out the lack of connection between us that still was unable to find expression in words. Silence.

Reflecting on Dennis that evening, I wrote in my journal:

How important it is for this boy to own his cultural roots; he cannot just push them aside. Should I mention to him that he is Chinese? Or should I wait for him to tell me?

With Dennis, I decided to wait. I recalled Irene de Castillejo's concept of meeting:

We are exhausted when talking to other people if we do not meet them, when one or both of us are hiding behind screens.
When we are fortunate enough to meet someone, . . . both are refreshed, for something has happened. It is as though a door had opened, and life suddenly takes on new meaning. For there to be a meeting, it seems as though a third, a something else, is always present. You may call it Love.
(de Castillejo, 1974, p. 11)

Both teacher and student are fortunate when a meeting occurs such as de Castillejo describes. I wondered if Dennis would ever come to trust me enough so he would no longer have to hide behind a screen.

The Language Center

The school where Dennis had his first Western English-speaking experience was in a Department of Housing and Urban Development (DHUD) project in a city near San Francisco, California. Over 50 percent of the students in that project lived with single parents. Most of these families received federal assistance through the Aid to Families with Dependent Children (AFDC) program. The school served approximately 180 children: 22 percent Filipino, 21 percent Hispanic, 21 percent Samoan, 17 percent African American, 7 percent Asian, 7 percent white, and 5 percent other.

The teachers in the school were tenured teachers in a two-school district. The teachers' union would not allow them to be replaced by untenured, bilingual teachers. Economic difficulties in the district had caused a semi-retired superintendent to be relegated to the position of principal, and he acted only as a figurehead. In essence, the teachers were the administrators of the school.

An attempt had been made to hire bilingual assistants, but it became difficult for school staff to find enough hours to teach, administrate, and also train assistants from the community. What was needed was a full-time professional bicultural teacher to work directly with all the immigrant children. That became my position. It was meant to be a "pull-out" program whereby the children came to me for periods of time from their own home classrooms.

The immigrant children entrusted to my care were from Mexico, El Salvador, Samoa, China, Hong Kong, Vietnam, and the Philippines. These children, ages 10 to 12, were considered "language minority" and were all immigrants.

Generally speaking, not all so-called language minority children are immigrants; but in my work with these particular children, I needed to address the unique phenomenon of their having been uprooted. Understanding and respecting the immigrants' native cultural attitude was as important as helping them learn a second language. I felt it was necessary to understand the trauma the children may have experienced in the chaos of the immigration process: culture shock, fears, the sudden inability to communicate, and the loss of the homeland.

Recollections of My Own Immigrant Experience

The child's unique perspective on immigration and second language literacy was well known to me. In my encounter with Dennis, I recalled my own uprooting experiences—to South America as a 5-year-old, and to the United States as a 13-year-old. Serious reflection about these experiences gave me a sense of what my immigrant students were feeling. I sought to give them what I would have liked teachers to have given me.

As a kindergarten-age child in a school in Colombia, South America, I felt uprooted from the known warmth and familiar images of my native country. Although I spoke the language of the new country, I needed the closeness of a teacher; I needed friends; I needed to be taken by the hand and shown how to use the pencil and write my name. I recall staring at a blank piece of paper, feeling inadequate and at a loss. I convinced my parents that school was too painful and that home was a safer place.

When I was a 13-year-old immigrant child in America, I again felt uprooted and had a deep sense of loss, missing familiar signs, friendships, and customs. Even though I was able to speak English well, I withdrew into silence because of culture shock. I withdrew even farther when I was surrounded by English-speaking children. They requested me to "Speak! Say something!" They meant well, but silence was my response.

"Are you an Indian?" they asked.

So as not to have my classmates mistake my identity—instead, to have them accept me—I made a pronounced attempt to conceal my accent. "What do you want me to say?"

"She speaks English!" I was overwhelmed that they hadn't realized I spoke English. I wondered why that was so unusual.

They flooded me with a deluge of questions, which, to my childish perspective, revealed their lack of knowledge about my country. Why is it, I thought, that I knew more about their country than they did about mine? I felt isolated. Soon thereafter, I asked my mother to have my hair curled because my traditional Asian bobbed haircut might be causing the other kids to see me as an Indian. I began to lose the sense of who I was in the thrall of their projections.

In the Philippines, we customarily greet each other with a kiss on the cheek; in America, we greet each other with a handshake or less. Each time I encountered an unexplained cultural difference such as this, I would feel awkward, confused, ashamed, or inadequate. The innumerable differences had nothing to do with language, because I was raised bilingually. I was more affected by the sense of cultural difference; loss of cultural identity and feelings of inadequacy would well up within me as I sat in class. I felt an unexplained void, an emptiness inside. I read well. I could illustrate. But these were mere skills. What I needed was a cultural connection. I was constantly adapting to the system. I needed the system to meet me halfway, to collaborate, to include my thoughts and feelings.

A School within a School

Was Dennis having a similar identity confusion to that which I experienced as an immigrant child? Certainly, his discarding of his cultural identity was visible. What were his inner feelings and thoughts, I wondered? How could I guide him to bridge the gap between his world and the new world? In the past, Italian, Greek, Russian, and Polish children went through the school system and were transformed into American kids. They all looked, talked, and acted like mainstream Americans. (However, the pain and confusion of feeling ashamed of their parents and grandparents have not been sufficiently documented in college texts; these emotions have been described in poignant novels and films.) Was Dennis trying to be like the others? How could he, when the school was so diverse?

Dennis's silence provided me with enough information to begin to design a program for him. My first encounter with him took place while the classroom was still empty, and he was the first of twenty immigrant children to meet with me. I also became acquainted with the other children assigned to the program, either alone (as with Dennis) or in cultural groups. I observed them carefully in order to structure a classroom to encompass all their needs. Because the room would be their center, a "school within a school," I felt it should be a place in which each and all could feel as comfortable as if they were at home in their countries of origin.

I had noticed that each child instinctively gravitated to an area in the classroom where he or she was comfortable. Dennis appeared to favor introversion and went to a quiet corner of the room. This would become the designated corner for silent work. I enclosed the area with a cardboard partition. It was a place for listening to stories on cassette and enjoying privacy.

Different cultures have different norms, values, worldviews, and expectations. These shape their members' patterns of individual and collective behavior. Although an entire culture also can express itself in an introverted or extroverted way (Wilson, 1988), individuals can move beyond a collective way of behaving when they begin to integrate other cultural ways within themselves. The most culturally alive people, says Henderson (1984), are those who are changing and recombining new attitudes all their lives.

In my work with immigrant children, I have become aware that each student's response and behavior in my classroom and out in the yard are a result of the complex interaction of his or her cultural background, individual nature, and length of time that student has been in the host country. When I speak of a group of children behaving in a certain way, my intentions are not meant to stereotype but to present what I have observed. For instance, when the Filipino and Hispanic students entered the classroom, it was evident by their chatter that they had been in the host country for some time. I arranged their desks in a cluster to accommodate their extroverted nature. When the Samoan children came in, they scoffed at the desks and sat on the floor in the far corner of the room. "Desks, desks, I hate desks," one of them said. So I brought in a large rug and placed it on the very spot where they sat; then I surrounded the area with a tree and some plants. I created an "island" to remind them of their homeland.

Because Dennis seemed so alone, I wanted to find a way to encourage him to come forward and relate to others. I had set up an art table in the middle of the room where children could express themselves nonverbally when they needed a break from the task of learning a second language. A filmstrip-making table set up at the opposite end of the quiet corner served for story writing and held a filmstrip projector for viewing. I also created a place with a table and two chairs where I could have a dialogue with each child one-to-one. I provided each child with a box in which to put confidential work or precious objects; this would give each child a sense of ownership and safety (see diagram on facing page).

Dennis Starts Work in His New Classroom

Children are very vulnerable to the projections of others—they look at another child and see their own face staring back at them. Children need mirroring. If a child looks into a friend's or a teacher's eyes and sees reflected someone who is not himself, he begins to lose his sense of self and to pattern himself on that "other." For that reason I planned to spend time with Dennis one-to-one for a brief period every day. In this way I could observe him closely and reflect on my observations in my personal journal. I would get to know Dennis, so he could begin to express his true self without fear that I would judge him.

In his first work day at the Center, Dennis showed he understood simple stories when I read aloud to him. I asked him questions and he pointed to the answers. In a quiet corner of the room, I surrounded him with stories in which humans triumph over wolves and giants. Marie Louise Von Franz (1970) speaks of storytelling as the international language of all ages, of all races and cultures. The universal themes found in good literature give children a sense of solidarity with all people. They transcend cultural attitudes. If Dennis felt powerless and alone, then these stories of heroes conquering dangerous animals or gigantic demons could give him a sense that he could prevail over his new environment. I was hoping he would identify with the heroes in these stories.

I wondered if Dennis had in any way picked up the previous teacher's attitude that he was a "problem." I needed to convey to him that I knew he was a child learning a new language and culture, a person in process, not a person with a problem.

When that first hour was over Dennis returned to his classroom, but three seconds later he was back at my door. Evidently we had begun to make some connection.

Because the "mainstream" children of the school were all reading from basal readers, I thought I would introduce Dennis to the same series so he would feel some commonality with the other children.

Diagram of the Center

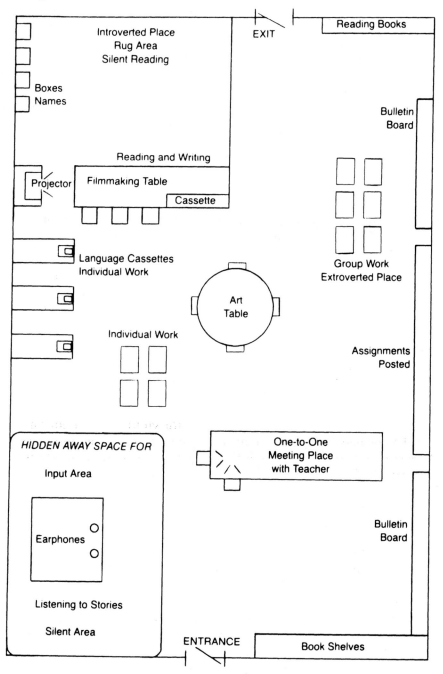

Also, coming from the traditional highly structured school system in China, he would feel some comfort by keeping to the same structure as the others. Starting from the first grade level of the series, Dennis could work as hard and long as he wished to move ahead. He could measure his own progress. It would give him the added experience of the cumulative aspects of a language, which we often take for granted. I would also motivate him to read through other literature-based reading books and tapes. Starting from the ground up, he could begin to transfer the literacy skills he had learned in his homeland.

At the conclusion of the second hour Dennis returned to his classroom, but in a few minutes he was at my door for a third time. He stood waiting to come in. I set up a plan for him to work on his own, including simple comprehension questions about the story he was reading, time for listening to stories, printing, and artwork. Because Dennis had had some schooling in China, I could help him learn to transfer the skills learned in his old school and use them on his own. I had already seen that Dennis was efficient by nature. Now he began to move about the room with a sense of belonging.

Dennis returned for a fourth hour, but by that time his energy and concentration seemed to fade; I decided to walk him reassuringly back to his regular classroom. I asked the teacher to involve him as much as possible with the others and asked that he not be tested or graded until he showed he was ready. The teacher agreed. This became Dennis's schedule for the day.

Each day as we worked together, I observed Dennis's gradual development. He had already mastered the alphabet. I then used the first level of the Ginn reading series, and we communicated through illustrations and gestures. I drew nouns and acted out verbs. He showed interest. I put a noun card down on the table followed by a verb card. Dennis read the words in a shy whisper. I spoke naturally and constantly monitored the cadence of my speech. I worked to maintain a natural rhythm of language so as not to be condescending, because even after only a year in the host country, there is much that a child comprehends in spite of his silence.

I taped the stories from his reader with him at my side so he could listen to them at home. I showed him how to use the vocabulary cards (flash cards consisting of words in the story that depicted the meaning through pictures) I had made for independent study. I also showed him how he could make his own cards. In the course of my work with him, I adapted the phonetic approach for sounding out words to suit his needs. Sometimes I did this in the context of the story, sometimes separately. I kept in mind that in transferring from Chinese characters to letters of the English alphabet, from one language to another, it is necessary for the child to be able to sound out new words to have a sense of his own power and not to feel dependent on the teacher. For the student who has already learned another alphabet, the use of phonics will help in transferring his or her old system into the English alphabet.

The Other Children at the Center

As some students engaged in independent work, I attended to the other students. They could not be treated as a homogenous group. The children varied in grade level from five through eight, and some, like Dennis, were recent arrivals. The students came to me at different times throughout the day, one or two from each class, with a maximum of twelve to fourteen at a time. I listened to the children attentively and tried to meet their individual needs. The Center was an exciting place. In fact, children from other classrooms wanted to know how they could join. To give the uprooted children at the Center an added sense of security, other children were allowed in only at the invitation of the immigrants.

Every day children came to the Center, as we all called the classroom we had designed. The children were busily occupied with each other or working on individual tasks. Each child in the program had a special place on the board where I wrote the particular assignments for the day. I worked with recent arrivals individually for 20 minutes daily so they would not feel lost. With the others, I worked in groups.

At the Center it was safe for the children to make mistakes. This eliminated any fear of being ridiculed. I made sure they knew they did not need to feel shame or reluctance to speak. The environment was friendly, with continued positive reinforcement. In correcting the papers of those who could write, I counted only the number correct rather than the number wrong.

I gave them as much content as they could handle. After all, if children are given too much new material, they cannot digest it psychically. Watching their bodies, listening to what they were saying, I could tell how much material to give them, for I believed that their curious minds would come back for more when they were ready. I did not want to rush the learning process, for doing so would initiate the sense that they were behind and needed to catch up. I wanted them to know they were free to grow slowly in their own good time.

My intention was to balance mainstreaming with "nesting" (I've taken this word from a drawing done by an immigrant child, who showed a nest and wrote that she needed a protected place to rest, to settle in, and to flourish). The balance of mainstreaming and nesting seemed to preclude what Henderson (1984) calls the two dangers: that of too much individuality and that of too much collectivity.

I designed individual assignments that were challenging and encouraged the children to reach their highest potential. The assignments were clear and concise, so the children knew exactly what to do each day. The balance of structure, certainty, and freedom at the Center was meant to strengthen their sense of security. The children competed only with themselves and not with others; this approach was chosen to give each immigrant child a feeling of success and to begin to heal the feeling of uprootedness.

There was a scheduled time for each child to come to the Center; but any time an immigrant child was overwhelmed by his or her regular classroom, he or she could find shelter in the support and freedom of the Center. To keep the children from cutting themselves off completely from their own classrooms, I limited visits to three a day. I also carefully monitored the student-teacher ratio. This flexibility enabled the students to express their desires and allowed me to control the number of students to suit the individual needs of the children without sacrificing my own ability to attend to them. This empowered me as well as the children. The homeroom teacher could send a child to me when she sensed his or her disorientation or frustration. When the child made one of these visits, he or she would check the board and continue the assignment independently or with a group. Later in this book I describe in detail the specific methodologies I created to help each child to develop a sense of personal power—and thus to learn.

The Power of Creative Expression

When Dennis had finished the first-level readers, I asked him to use his new vocabulary to write a paragraph or two. Without resistance, he managed to come up with an interesting story. I went over it with him, showing him the structure of the written word. He observed attentively. It was at this moment that an inspiration struck me. This was his very own story, I thought. If he could make a filmstrip illustrating the story and read it onto a cassette tape, then he could see his illustrations on a screen and we could hear his voice. This could be the method that would break his silence. Dennis and I would view the story. Then he could share it with a friend, and as he gained confidence, with the group.

I showed Dennis how to illustrate his story with felt-tip pens on a filmstrip. He took all the materials home. Because I was close to exceeding my school budget, I brought some old records from my garage to show Dennis how to enhance his filmstory with background music. And we would include sound effects. For instance, we used a spoon striking a glass to indicate when to move on to the next frame.

The next morning, when Dennis was about to come for his lesson, I was working matter-of-factly in the film-making corner. I expected him to enter the room in his usual serious manner; instead, the door flew open and a wide-eyed Dennis exclaimed with an exuberance that finally broke his long silence: "I made a cartoon, I made a cartoon!" There was a contagious smile on his face. I wanted to respond with a hug, but, wishing to respect his innate cultural reserve, I thought it best to wait. I smiled in return.

Gingerbread

Dennis and I sat together on the carpet. Bringing out the old records, I asked him to listen and select the background music to suit his story. In no time he selected a very lively piece of classical music. I went through the step-by-step process of making the film: music, loud, soft; speak; make sound effects; signal by striking the glass; move to the next frame. He got it! He motioned me to go away, and he worked on the film by himself. When he had finished, he beckoned me to come and see it. Here is a reproduction of his filmstrip entitled *Gingerbread*. This was the first time I heard him speak out.

■ *Gingerbread*

START

One day, Gingerbread went outside of the house to play.

He ran to the park to play with the swings.

Then he went to get his bicycle.

On the way home, he saw a baby bird fall down
(drop sound), oh!

He went home. He ate lunch (munching sound).

It was Christmas time.

Santa Claus give his presents.

Then he open the box, he said, "What's in there?"
It was a toy cat.

"Oh," he said, "I like this cat."

He said, "Thanks, Santa Claus."

He looked out the window and saw snow.

He went outside to play.

Then he made one snowman.

Then he went to play in the hills.

When he finished, he went home very tired.

After his shower, he fell asleep.

The End.

With genuine enthusiasm, I applauded the story. Because Dennis responded favorably to my energetic response, I asked him to select a classmate to see the film. I wanted to build on the rapport between us and widen his friendships. Looking around the room, he pointed to a boy from the Philippines. As both boys sat together viewing the filmstrip, I wondered what might be the significance of the fallen bird, the presents, the tired feelings. (Often the children at the Center would fall asleep behind the cardboard partition.) I knew he was expressing more than just a story about a gingerbread. It revealed to me much more than his command of grammar and syntax. There was hope in the story, and he was opening up to the world—coming out of his isolation into a world perceived as friendly. The story seemed to portray a carefree, enjoyable life that was not totally characteristic of Dennis. Was it wishful thinking, I wondered.

The process of drawing and illustrating became Dennis's medium of communication and self-expression. He eventually became friends with the boy from the Philippines, who also applauded his filmstrip story. Together they began to write other stories. Dennis began to externalize his fears, dealing with them symbolically. Wickes (1966) points out that symbols reflect our deep inner selves, and that children who have an abundance of fantasy seem to be especially connected to this interior level of experience.

Near the Mountain

Dennis wrote a second filmstrip shortly after *Gingerbread*, entitled *Near the Mountain*.

■ **Near the Mountain**

START

Near the Mountain

One day my friend and I went walking in the mountain.

We were so tired, we sat down on the ground.

Soon it was night time.

Then we saw two yellow eyes.

We went to the yellow eyes.

And it was gone.

We went to look and look. It was a tiger.

Then the tiger was chasing us.

We ran so fast from the tiger. (gasps)

And soon morning came.

Then I saw a house near the mountain.

We went inside.

And we saw a woman in the house.

She was cooking something.

My friend said, "I am so hungry."

And the woman saw us.

I said, "Can we go in?"

The woman said, "Oh, sure."

And the woman let us eat some cookies.
(eating sound)

After, a man came home. We said to the man, "We saw a tiger near the mountain."

At night time, the man saw the tiger. He shot the tiger and the tiger was dead.

The End.

Thank you.

In the filmstrip is an old couple with a house in which Dennis and his friend take refuge. It is significant that in the first story Dennis was alone in the experience of life and in the second story he had a friend, even though he had not yet established a friendship with anyone in the Center. Those images—the fallen bird, the staring yellow eyes of a tiger—brought back feelings of my own uprooting experience. Every immigrant has a story to tell, and I wondered what Dennis's might be as he continued to open up through the process of communicating through filmstrip stories.

Children in the class began to ask to see Dennis's stories, and he efficiently set up the filmstrip projector. His voice, timid at first, became increasingly confident as his peers and I loudly applauded the stories. Through this medium he began to develop socially. The stories were clearly an expression of himself. At the Center he could move safely from the known to the unknown and begin to integrate his two isolated cultural experiences—of China and of America.

Dennis Discovers His True Self

Dennis wrote several other stories during his two years at the Center. He even taught the other children how to make filmstrip stories. In Asia, it is customary for younger children to respect the older one. He took this responsibility seriously. I was usually called in to help with the final recording so that my professional expertise would ensure that the novice would produce a polished piece of work and that no one would laugh at his or her first attempt. I also gathered the children together to drum up ideas for sound effects. How original were the sounds they made! Laughter often broke out, but it was friendly laughter.

Dennis read daily, learned to listen to and discuss the stories, continued to write, and spent time at the art table. It was obvious to me that he was not only watching cartoons at home but listening to the news as well. Often his paragraphs expressed knowledge of world events or news of the day, as in his paragraph and illustration of the medfly, a pest that was infesting California at the time.

Dennis   Sept /29/81

This is a medfly, and it is 400 years old. It has many friends. It likes to fight sometimes!

One day, the medfly was flying and it saw the fruits, so it went down and started to eat. Then a man saw a hole in all the fruits. He took the medicine and started to kill the medfly. The medfly was dead.

The End

After Dennis broke out of his isolation and silence, he progressed rapidly. On one occasion his homeroom teacher expressed amusement that he had tapped her on the shoulder one day and told her he would take the history test. Later, unable to contain her excitement, she stopped by to say he had gotten an A on the test.

The Wolf

Dennis's final filmstrip still contained the elements of fear and safety that characterized his previous filmstrips, but a new maturity was also evident. His voice was strong and confident, conveying a "thank you" to everyone. Even more significant was the fact that for the first time in the two years I had been working with Dennis, his name appeared in Chinese. This was indeed a change, a triumph for us all. When he asked me to view his story before he presented it to his classmates, I could not help but notice the Chinese characters on the second frame. I said nothing, although I noticed how he looked at me from the side; but I let the film move on to the next frame as I had done with the others. Silence. I contained the exuberance I felt.

■   **The Wolf**

START

The Wolf

by Dennis

One day, I was flying a kite in the field.

I ran so fast and the kite flew up.

I was so happy. Then I fell down. The kite was flying away.

Then I went down the hill to look.

And I saw a wolf coming after me.

I was very scared. (sound)

Then I ran very fast from the wolf. I ran
and ran and ran. (running sounds)

Then I ran down the hill.

And I saw a house. I was running to the
house. (running sounds)

Then I shut the door. (bang)

The wolf scratched the door.

I closed the door very hard.

After, I heard something coming.

Then, I heard the gun sound. (bang)

After, I opened the door.

I saw a man got the wolf.

And I said to the man, "Thank you for help-ing me."

I was very happy and I ran home.

The End.

Thank everybody.

Not long after the "man got the wolf" with a "gun sound," Dennis showed his newfound happiness "and ran home." Perhaps he was at home with himself. I saw him at the art table quietly decorating what I thought was a design. He was enhancing it with glue and glitter. It attracted my attention, so I looked over his shoulder. I asked what it might be and he responded in a slightly defensive manner, "My name."

Dennis's Name

Intrigued and fascinated, the other children rushed over to the table for a look. They asked Dennis to write their names in Chinese as well. He wrote each of their names, using Chinese characters, and these were hung around the room in appreciation of an old skill renewed.

Classmates' Names (Alex and Miguel) in Chinese Characters

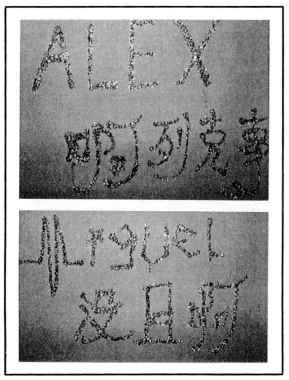

One week before graduation, as I entered the Center early one morning, the room still empty, I noticed a beautifully designed poster on the art table. On it was a message in two languages: "Dennis is alive."

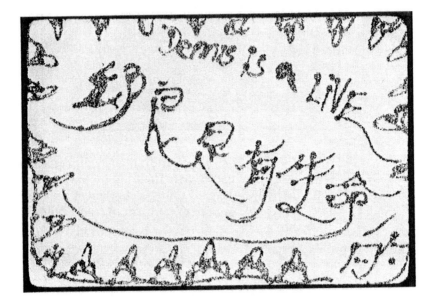

"Alive" in Dennis's Chinese version was written as "Qiu Liang is full of energy and curiosity." At last Dennis not only revealed his true self and cultural identity but was able to show the amount of energy he had kept pent up inside. I took the poster and hung it up in the room. There it stayed until graduation. No comment was made, just silent validation.

On graduation day I met him in the corridor. He spontaneously rushed up and embraced me with a lot of energy and life. I knew then that he would be fine. Dennis is alive! Qiu Liang is full of life energy!

Summary

Dennis had at first pushed away the pencil and refused to write his real name in Chinese. In essence he was trying to push aside his cultural self. Uprooted from his country and surrounded by an unfamiliar environment, he was silent.

As Dennis began to feel safe at the Center, and with regular cultural, academic, and psychological interventions, his true self began to emerge and Qiu Liang came alive!

The following guidelines recapitulate what worked with Qiu Liang and suggest ways of working with immigrant children who hide themselves from a world to which they wish to belong:

Establish a feeling of home outside the student's home.

Allow space for the student's precious objects.

Notice the spaces in the room where the child feels comfortable, and make them available to the child.

Use storytelling and the themes of heroes with whom the child can identify.

Read books that encourage cumulative language development as well as those with a phonetic approach—a *both/and* rather than an *either/or* approach.

Use gestures, illustrations, and dramatic filmstrip-making.

Tape stories from the child's reader for independent work.

Correct papers with a focus on the number correct rather than the number wrong.

Show the child how to transfer a previously developed ability in reading and writing into a new form and new alphabet—the additive learning of a language.

Work with each child from 15 to 20 minutes daily so that cultural identity is maintained and you can monitor progress.

Give the child challenging material. Do not rush the process, but help the child to reach his or her potential.

Enable the child to compete academically with himself/herself and not with other students, keeping in mind that the child will eventually want to join the "mainstream" students.

Help the child gain confidence academically to succeed in the "mainstream" classes where grades are given competitively.

Use the child's cultural attitude of valuing the importance of the "older one" to encourage sharing with others what he or she has learned.

Balance "nesting" and "mainstreaming."

Make assignments clear, balancing structure and freedom.

Spend three entire periods on ESL listening, reading vocabulary-building texts for in-depth learning, and language mastery, for students to gain closer relationships with the teacher.

Honor the child's original or native name and language.

2

The Phenomenon of
Uprooting

I felt different from everyone else. . . . I couldn't really be with anybody because they couldn't understand me and I couldn't understand them. There was no way I could try to make things better for myself. It was hard just feeling bad.

I felt it was hard for me to tell them all that I felt, express it all; so I just kept some feelings inside myself.

IMMIGRANT CHILDREN FROM CHINA,
AGES 10 AND 11

The stages I describe in this chapter have been formulated largely on the basis of my own observations, experience, dialogues with children and parents, and review of the literature. These descriptions are general representations, but they are not universally true for all children. Stages may occur simultaneously or in varying degrees.

Understanding the Silent Stage

If there is one characteristic of the uprooting experience that appears to be shared by all immigrant children irrespective of nationality, economic status, family stability, or any other factor, it is the silent stage when the children experience the school culture as different from their own and when their inability to communicate with peers is caused by a language or cultural difference.

In the silent stage, immigrant children may appear to be retiring, moody, fearful, even terrified. Yet their silence is not an indication that they are unwilling to socialize or cooperate. I have found that immigrant children long to blend in with other children, to join in their activities, but their emotions and fears hold them back. To get through the period of adjustment in which these feelings are dominant, the immigrant child adopts the mechanism of silence. It is important during this time to help the child find ways to communicate—verbally, in writing, or through art. The phase may last from one to two years or more if the child finds no connection in friendships or with teachers.

The silent stage need not be a negative experience; it may even have advantages. While some children are trapped in helpless silence by their inability to communicate in the dominant language, they become insightful observers of their own human condition and of life around them. In that silence, they develop strong listening skills. They come to value keenly language as a mode of self-expression; they do not take language for granted because of the time in their lives when they were silent. Then they experience the sheer joy of breaking that silence. The rich life experience, history, and traditions embodied in their own language are a wealth of knowledge they have been waiting to share; they can finally do so when they break out of the silence through speech, writing, or art.

I regard the silent stage as a period of incubation during which the child must be provided with a warm and nurturing environment that makes it safe for him or her eventually to break out of a shell as well as to accept himself or herself as belonging to a diverse society. Ultimately, supporting the child through this crucial period is more efficient than the "sink-or-swim" approach of placing the child into the "mainstream." Moving the child from class to class to speed up the learning of English often has the unintentional effect of making the child relive the uprooting experience again and again.

The Uprooting Experience

In the uprooting experience, survival instincts are awakened. The farther apart the cultural attitudes of the child's original country and the host country, the more intense are these emotions. Qiu Liang (Dennis), for instance, grew up in an Eastern communist society that was, generally speaking, introverted, and he was thrust into a generally extroverted, Western, heterogeneous capitalist society. He had to wrestle with the opposite worlds within himself. Therefore, the experience was more intense for him than for the other immigrant children who had been exposed to Western cultures.

Even though immigrant children have left behind their systems of communication, their cultural beliefs, and the cultural identity that once gave meaning to their lives, the psychological traumas of uprooting are less visible and less easily measured than their language proficiency. This is especially true of catastrophically uprooted children who arrived in America during the 1974–1975 exodus from Vietnam (Sokoloff, Carlin, and Pham, 1984).

When a child is uprooted from all signs of the familiar and is transported to an unfamiliar foreign land, he or she may experience some degree of shock. This culture shock is much the same as the shock we observe in a plant when a gardener transplants it from one soil to another. We know that shock occurs in plants, but we are not always conscious of the effects of such transplants on children. Some plants survive, often because of the gardener's care; some children survive because of a teacher, peers, or a significant person who nurtures them during the transition toward integration into a new social milieu. The silent stage in school is the result of culture shock, which has its origins in the uprooting phenomenon.

Culture Shock

Culture shock is precipitated by the anxiety that results from losing all familiar signs and symbols of social intercourse (Oberg, 1960). Every culture has subtle, if not unconscious, signs by which people evaluate what they say and do. Losing these cues produces strain, uneasiness, and even emotional maladjustment if the person is received badly, because the props have been swept away and there is no longer a familiar foundation on which to stand. Until one learns the cues of the new culture, one is culturally disoriented (Smalley, 1963). Thus, the silence.

In the study of anthropology, we learn that the feelings and thoughts one is used to, as well as the behavior and rules imposed and accepted by members of a cultural group, are "normal." It is when we look at culture shock as "abnormal" that we set ourselves up to believe that one group is better than another. To ease culture shock in no way means that one has to assimilate quickly and become what one is not; rather, one should stay connected to one's own culture and also learn the cues of the new culture—a both/and experience. In the transplant, it is customary for the gardener to take as many of the plant's roots as possible to the new ground. In the uprooting experience, the child's family must do the same. Teachers as "gardeners" of these seedlings need to understand the importance of cultural roots.

It is normal for children to experience cultural disorientation when uprooted from their country and placed in a different environment, just as it is normal for plants to wilt a little while being transplanted and while the roots are strengthening and expanding in new soil.

During the "transplant" of immigrant children, parents and/or relatives may experience homesickness, grief, uncertainty about the future, and frustration as they attempt to find meaningful work and establish themselves in the new country. This anxiety is usually picked up by the child, often unbeknown to the parent or extended family members. Some children experience transplantation without the comforting presence of their parents, either because relatives or extended family are in charge at home or because the children have been sent abroad to live with relatives.

In low-income immigrant families, it may be difficult for parents to nurture their children fully because the uprooting experience itself saps the parents' energy (Chao and Sung, 1977). The adults in the household may have to work many hours a day. The adult undergoing culture shock has experience, age, and some ability to know what it takes to get over the disorientation, but the child often has a sense of helplessness. When the adults also feel despair about the change in their material and physical circumstances and worry about coping in the new environment, their feelings are often communicated unconsciously to the child, who then feels truly helpless.

> *There is no way that I could try to make things better for myself. It's hard just feeling bad.*
> IMMIGRANT CHILD FROM CHINA

Often the schools are held responsible for nurturing children who have been left to fend for themselves while parents work, or who spend more time at school than with their families. For many children, the language barrier is formidable (Chao and Sung, 1977). When a teacher understands the causes of these strong emotions and can look into the child's inner world and know the reason for the silence, then he or she may be able to identify what type of support the child needs to emerge from the silence. The teacher may be able to guide the child in transforming negative emotions to positive, more life-enhancing energy. In a study of 300 children ages 5 to 8 (Milner, 1983), immigrant minority children were shown dolls or pictures representing both their racial group and Anglos. In response, 58 per-

cent of West Indian children and 45 percent of Asian children maintained that the doll that looked like them was "bad." Eighty-two
percent of the West Indians and 77 percent of the Asians also said the
doll that looked like them was "ugly." Milner concluded that immigrant minority children tend to devalue their own ethnic group.

Stages of Uprooting

Mixed Emotions

During the first stage of uprooting, the child is told by the parents
that he or she will be moving to another country. For many children
the announcement is made the day before, two days before, a week
earlier, or even earlier than that, depending on family circumstances.
At first the child feels a lot of excitement or fear about the journey,
mixed with sadness at leaving best friends, parents, siblings, acquain-
tances, grandparents, or other relatives. There is not much time to
deal with feelings, as the move usually is sudden and plans for trans-
portation and the mechanics of departure take up most of the time.
Finally, the exodus begins.

> *I was born in Afghanistan in a beautiful home. I lived there for five
> years. I went to school in Afghanistan up to second grade. I was
> eight. Then the Russians came so we had to move from Afghani-
> stan to Pakistan. . . . I started school third grade in Pakistan.*
>
> *One day my mom came and said, "We are going to Amer-
> ica." I was really shocked because she never told us that we were
> going to America. So we came.*
>
> BOY FROM AFGHANISTAN, AGE 11

> *I felt sad when I had to leave. I was crying because I would not
> be able to ride horses, swim, or be with my friends. My mom and
> I were both crying.*
>
> BOY FROM MEXICO, AGE 10½

> *I felt sad and happy. I felt sad to leave my friends behind and
> happy to go to a new place.*
>
> BOY FROM MEXICO, AGE 11

I observed one child from Mexico who was well received in a Spanish bilingual classroom, surrounded by friends. On the outside all
seemed well, but upon closer examination she revealed her depression:

> *I had to leave Mexico with my family. I was told the day before
> that I had to pack. I feel bad and depressed because I left my*

best friend behind. They tell me I must write to her or she will get sick.

GIRL FROM MEXICO, AGE 11½

Similarly, another girl wrote about her inner feelings:

I knew for two years that my family was planning to go to the United States. I came home from a fiesta late one night and I saw my mother packing. She said that the papers finally came and we were leaving the next morning. We packed until early morning. That was confusing and sad because I never got to say goodbye to my friends.

GIRL FROM MEXICO, AGE 12

Excitement or Fear in the Adventure of the Journey

In the second stage of uprooting, the child is on a train, car, plane, boat, camel, or on foot. He or she is usually with a parent or relative, and perhaps siblings, and there is much discussion among the family in their own language. Some families make numerous intermediate stopovers for different lengths of time in several different countries. Others come directly to the host country. During the journey, the child experiences excitement and adventure. If the child comes from a war-torn country or has left for political, religious, or economic reasons, a lot of fear and anxiety—even silence or danger—exist during the journey. The child may be in shock, pain, or trauma over the loss of a parent or other close family members or friends. One Vietnamese boy described the fear he experienced when he left his homeland under dangerous conditions:

When I was little in Vietnam, at the age of nine I fled the country by boat to reach the shores of Malaysia.

Before I came here, everybody sat in a little boat. We went to sea and we came to a big boat. At that time, everybody push, push everybody because they wanted to go in the boat first. I couldn't push because everybody was big. I was scared. I was thinking that maybe I couldn't get in the boat. I was with my uncle and my sister. She was eleven years old.

I did get in the boat. The first day in the boat, the police in another boat came and asked what we were doing and where we were going. My uncle told all the kids to go under in the boat. He told the police that we were going fishing. Then the police let us go.

When I was under inside the boat, I felt scared because if they knew we were not going fishing and they catch us, we

*would go to prison. They lock us up. There were 26 or 30 people
in the boat.*

BOY FROM VIETNAM, AGE 11

Curiosity

The third stage of uprooting occurs when the child arrives in the
new country. Sometimes relatives are there to greet the family; sometimes not. If the family is fortunate, a relative has gone ahead so they
can arrive at a home (furnished or unfurnished). If they are refugees,
they may have spent time in refugee camps and made many moves,
sometimes to relatives' homes where everyone lives in cramped conditions. The child has many unsettled feelings, at times unknown to the
adults, but communication among the family or extended family is
ongoing. The child gains emotional support from being together with
familiar adults, usually other family members, and becomes curious
about things that are different from home. Once the child or family
begins to settle down, the transplant begins.

*This is my strength. My father came to the United States first.
He found a job and sent us money. We came by plane to Los
Angeles. At first we lived with my uncle. Then my father looked
for an apartment. Then we went to Oakland. From there we went
to San Leandro and then we went to Hayward. Our apartment is
not big, but it is comfortable. We are away from bad people.
From my point of view, I have a good, loving family and I am
happy.*

GIRL FROM MEXICO, AGE 10
(translated from Spanish)

*When I came to America, I was curious. I see many things. In
the grocery store I see the door open by itself. I see candies, so
many candies! I say, "Mom, look at the candies!"*

BOY FROM ROMANIA, AGE 11

Culture Shock: Depression and Confusion

During the fourth stage, if the child is of school age, plans are
made for schooling. He or she is now separated from the warmth of
family members and leaves to go to school. A child who does not
speak the language of the host country may experience varying degrees of culture shock, particularly if he or she is not well received.
The child may enter the silent stage, keeping his or her emotions
inside, including emotions stirred up in the native country during the

initial stage of moving. The child may become depressed or confused and let down. If the child compares himself or herself to the "mainstream" children, he or she may feel hopeless of ever catching up or belonging.

> *I want to stay close to my family, I am afraid to leave them, but I must go to school. It is hard to go into a classroom. It is new and I feel as if everyone is looking at me and staring at me.*
>
> *I was having a difficult time adjusting. I didn't like going to school. I was not sure I was going to make it. I couldn't speak English. I didn't understand what they were saying. I was scared, afraid to express the emotions.*
>
> BOY FROM CHINA, AGE 12

> *I was born in Mexico. When I first went to school in the U.S., I found everything very strange. I wanted to cry.*
>
> *Those first weeks we moved around exchanging classes. It was very confusing. I did not understand because the teacher never told me we were going to move from class to class. I did not know anyone. It took time to get used to school.*
>
> GIRL FROM MEXICO, AGE 11½
> (translated from Spanish)

Assimilation or Acculturation

During the fifth stage, the immigrant child faces pressure to assimilate into the new culture.

Assimilation, I think, forces people to become carbon-copy personalities, because the person has to give up cherished values and ways of behaving to become a part of the mainstream culture; *acculturation*, on the other hand, allows the individual to become part of the mainstream culture without discarding past meaningful traditions and values. I do agree with Bowers (1984) that people cannot exchange one culture for another in the same way that they exchange commodities. Western industrial societies are commodity oriented, and commodities are easily discarded and quickly replaced. Consciously or unconsciously, school professionals tend to transfer the commodity model onto that of culture, believing that children can discard their old cultural values and replace them with new ones as easily as they throw away their old shoes and get a new pair. In general, societies such as ours in the United States do not attempt to acculturate or integrate; rather, they assimilate immigrant children into the educational system and the society at large, says Bhatnager (1981).

During the fifth stage, the child may attempt to blend in and be like his or her peers; the child may assimilate and act as if the past never existed, denying his or her cultural self. If he or she can be helped by teachers to embrace both worlds, an integrated sense of self can develop and the child can make strides forward. If there is no intervention, either by teachers, other adults, or peers, the child may feel hopelessly shut off from his past and/or become stuck at that level. This stage is crucial; the child can either be guided to integrate his or her cultural self or be left alone to discard it, only to try to regain it in later life.

In the Mainstream

During the sixth stage, the child—ready or not—is in the mainstream. Children who have been successful at integrating or open about accepting their past with their present are now well adjusted and feel at home with themselves. They are said to be "grounded" and "well rounded"; the transplant is successful. When the child is able to own his or her cultural roots, he can begin to "transplant" successfully without shutting off or destroying his original cultural self.

In the story of Dennis (Qiu Liang), we can observe his initial attempt to push away his cultural self. He felt alive and whole when he revealed his Chinese name and then brought out his language for the world to see—he was no longer afraid. A sense of integration began to take place.

I have known children who were afraid to reveal their backgrounds for fear of discrimination or ridicule and who pushed their cultural past into the unconscious, or off onto their home life. These children feel uncomfortable, acting one way at school and another at home. Their maladjustment will manifest itself in a cultural split, which will continue as long as no intervention occurs. When they grow up, if they become conscious of their two separate worlds they may look down upon, reject, or deny their native cultures; or they may discover that native part of themselves left behind in childhood. When they try to regain this early self at the adult stage, integration of life will take time.

Understanding the Immigrant Child's Inner World

The immigrant child begins to clarify what is meant by the "inner world" when he says, "I felt it was hard for me . . . to express it all; so I just kept some feeling inside myself." He speaks here of his experiences, thoughts, feelings, and reactions contained, if not imprisoned, by the fear inside him.

The child's true feelings and thoughts are usually not what adults think they are. The inner world is the deeper area within the child that can be defined as the truth within (whether or not that "truth" has any basis in reality) or, simply, what the child feels and believes. For example, the child may feel that others are laughing at her for being "different," when in reality the children are laughing at something else. The inner world is where fears and unreasoning joyousness, fantasies, and intuition move and speak. "For us as adults," says Wickes (1966, p. vii), "it is a surprising world; the forgotten world of our own childhood where imaginary, grotesque, or obscure characters can influence the drama of self-creation or self-destruction."

Wickes (1988) establishes that children are deeply involved in the psychological attitude of their parents; what happens, then, if their parents' language, values, culture, and traditions are different from the language, culture, and traditions of the host country or the children's peers? Wickes says that loving, secure relationships with parents are important for children's growth and well-being. What happens when they sense their parents' insecurity, struggle for survival, and inability to find time to nurture, or if they think the parents' values are inferior to those of the new environment? Ada (1993, p. 158) addresses this issue:

> Schools can never be neutral in this regard. . . . The conscious or unconscious practices of the school, including its approach to literacy, serve to either validate or invalidate the home cultures, thus helping or hindering family relationships.

The filmstrip stories told by the children at the Center revealed some of their hidden experiences, thoughts, and emotions. It is natural for children to share what moves them deeply, because they feel more at home when both inner and outer worlds are in harmony. For example, when Qiu Liang finally got the courage to write his Chinese name in *The Wolf* story, both his worlds, inner and outer, were at one. Through the filmstrip stories the children revealed their inner world. Themes such as isolation, exhaustion, loneliness, confusion, cultural differences, and their struggle at school began to emerge.

As a teacher I was moved by the children's honesty and trust, which fostered my own desire to be genuine with them. Their artwork was full of meaning; the music they selected seemed to represent their feelings. Children who wrote sad stories selected melancholy music. Those who wrote about friends frolicking selected lively tunes. Wickes says in her Preface (1988, p. xiv):

> If we are to enter into the inner world of the child, then we must take with us two things: love and understanding. . . . It

is from the children themselves that we learn, and it is from their gifts to us that we grow in understanding.

Isolation

At the Center I worked with Alice, Qiu Liang's younger sister. The 10-year-old Alice was a disciplined student who followed directions, completed all assignments, and kept to herself. She could be counted upon to enter the room diligently, check the board for the day's work, and be off to complete the task of the morning: 10 minutes on the language master, 15 minutes of silent reading, 15 minutes of reading with the group. She was so methodical that a 12-year-old who had recently arrived from Mexico, Alejandro, observed in Spanish, *Me gusta como trabaja*: "I like how she works." Alejandro was friendly; Alice, distant and concentrated on her work. I reflected on the differences between these students. For Alejandro it was easy to relate because we both spoke Spanish. Alice was unusually serious and she isolated herself from the rest of the class, always on task.

I recalled my visit to Mainland China immediately after it had opened up to the Western world. I visited a classroom where the young children sat on straight-backed chairs in a circle, and the teacher stood by a flannel board with a pointer as the children recited by rote. The children sat erect, with their hands behind their backs, and responded in unison to mathematics questions. After 10 or 15 minutes the children were allowed to walk together quickly in a circle for a break. I noticed one little boy who made an attempt to skip away from the circle, but at the clearing of the teacher's throat he was back in line. The lessons were teacher-directed and the children were taught to focus on the classroom task. In the schoolyard at recess the children spontaneously climbed the jungle gym and played on the swings, but they were always clear about their limits and boundaries. Yard duty was not at all a chore for the teacher; rather, it was a period of quiet observation of children at play.

We were told by the teachers of the school that in China the children were taught to have a high regard, love, and respect for teachers because teachers were responsible for developing their minds. They were to love both parents and teachers, but teachers more; because although their parents had brought them into the world, their teachers would help them contribute their talents to the world. I relate this story not to characterize Chinese education on the basis of one visit but to share my reflections then and my desire to understand the environment Alice may have come from and the difficulties she would have been experiencing at a school such as ours where schoolyard cultural conflicts were a daily occurrence. For a thorough account of the Chinese educational system, I refer readers to the work of Liljestrom et al. (1982).

Alice seemed to respond to school. After a year in the host country she was articulate but preferred to speak only to me, disregarding the others. I wondered what she might be thinking or feeling. She came to the Center with a group of eight other children. Their teacher had allowed this group only one class period at the Center, so I worked with her in a group but from time to time listened to the stories she wrote about kittens and the Chinese New Year celebration.

It was not until her second year at the Center that Alice expressed a desire to write a filmstrip story, *The Little Banana*. Filmstrip storymaking had by this time developed into a procedure any student could choose. After a student initially wrote a story, the group gathered around the writer for the final draft. The group's task was to listen to the story, validate the things they liked only, and then work together as a team to come up with sound effects: *bang, bang, tick, tick, tweet, tweet, ssh, ssh, slurp, slurp.* The process of "validation only" was meant to build self-esteem. They were inwardly too critical of themselves already. They did not need more criticism.

Alice, although a superior student, had trouble making her filmstrip. She felt she needed permission to express herself freely. I wanted to make sure she was ready and that making the filmstrip was her own decision.

■ The Little Banana

START

The Little Banana

This is a little banana.

It lives in a city.

Every morning it likes to do some exercises.
(1, 2, 3, 4; 1, 2, 3, 4)

One day it went walking down the street.
(steps)

It saw an apple fall from the tree. (dropping sound)

It picked up the apple.

Then it brought the apple to its home.

The banana put the apple on the table.

It went to its room to change its clothes.

Then the banana brought the apple to the sink and started to wash it. (washing sounds)

Then it tasted the apple. (slurp, slurp)

It said, "I like this apple. I am going to get another."

Then the banana went to the apple tree again. (steps)

This time it saw another apple bigger than the last one.

and the banana was very happy.

The End

Alice's little banana lived in a city and liked to do its exercises every morning, a custom I had seen in China. So I began a drum-like beat and started keeping time as in a march: 1, 2, 3, 4; 1, 2, 3, 4. I led the group. Alice burst into laughter and everyone joined in. This was the first time I had seen her laugh. This child from Mao's China must have experienced profound differences in the school systems. And now, a teacher was marching around with the children! How absurd! The experience broke the ice of her isolation, and she began to relate to the other children.

Unlike her brother, Alice still called herself "Alice" at the end of her second year. She kept her Chinese name concealed. Having worked with her in a group for an hour of language arts daily, I found there was little she revealed verbally or through her artwork about her inner world or her past life in China. Persons who feel it necessary to keep such a fundamental part of their being concealed from the society they live in are isolated at the very root of their being, no matter how sociable they may appear to others.

Exhaustion

A recurring theme regarding the inner world of the immigrant child is a feeling of exhaustion, not only from the sounds of a new language but also from the continual parade of strange sights and events in a new culture. The opening of Qiu Liang's filmstrip about the tiger found two boys walking up the mountain and becoming "so tired we sat down on the ground." In a filmstrip by Cindy, a girl from Hong Kong, the main character becomes tired at the end of the story and goes to take a nap. Alejandro also used his filmstrip to show his falling asleep. All these filmstrips indicate that constant tiredness from having to pay so much attention to the language and images of the new country is a daily part of the immigrant child's experience.

Cindy was an inquisitive, highly motivated sixth grade student. After a year of mainstream schooling, she joined the Center for one class period per day. She worked in a small reading group with other children and, from time to time, individually with me. Sometimes she worked with a language master machine, reading aloud to herself and listening to her recorded voice. She was pleasant, articulate, and graceful. In her filmstrip she expresses her exhaustion.

■ The Upside Down Morning

START

The Upside Down Morning

One morning when I woke up, I saw the sun coming through my window.

It was going to be a good day, I thought.

When I went downstairs, everything was upside-down.

Wow! I was so hungry, I opened the refrigerator . . .

and things began falling down.

I went to the table to get a cup.

When I opened the faucet to get a drink, the water went right through my cup.

I started to go and take a walk around the block.

Well, I saw many more strange things.

I saw a horse riding in a car.

And I saw funny looking houses.

I saw fish swimming on sidewalks. Could you imagine, swimming on your sidewalk?

I saw bubbles coming out of the girl's head.

I saw a flower growing on top of a bird's back.

When I walked around one block, I saw a cat that had a mustache.

I was so scared I ran home.

I got tired from that walk. I went to take a nap.

When I woke up, everything was back to normal.

The End.

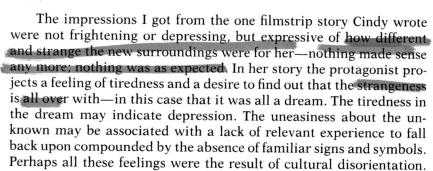

The impressions I got from the one filmstrip story Cindy wrote were not frightening or depressing, but expressive of how different and strange the new surroundings were for her—nothing made sense any more; nothing was as expected. In her story the protagonist projects a feeling of tiredness and a desire to find out that the strangeness is all over with—in this case that it was all a dream. The tiredness in the dream may indicate depression. The uneasiness about the unknown may be associated with a lack of relevant experience to fall back upon compounded by the absence of familiar signs and symbols. Perhaps all these feelings were the result of cultural disorientation.

Whenever I saw a child asleep at the listening center or on the blue rug, I would allow him or her the freedom to experience the tiredness and exhaustion and I would motion to the others to contain their giggles and get back to work. Sleep can be a way of shutting down the mind and possibly taking a rest from the task of learning a new language and from the struggles at home where the immigrant family is trying to adjust to a new environment, searching for a job, or feeling homesick.

It was moving to me that no one really took advantage of this freedom to sleep, because most of the children were involved at all times either individually or with the others. Only once, when one child emerged from a deep sleep, did I sense by the look on her face that she felt embarrassed and guilty about sleeping in class. To get the message across to her that following her instincts was natural after a long day's work wrestling with a second language, I pretended to take a nap on the very spot where she had fallen asleep. What I thought would result in classroom disorder by my "falling asleep on the job" actually resulted in a quiet and protective tenderness on the part of the children. "Ssh, quiet, teacher is asleep, get to work," I heard the "older one" say, and they got on with their work. The result of my experiment with "sleeping" confirmed what I had intuited—that the children were becoming less dependent on me and more in touch with their own sense of power. They were becoming more connected to each other.

Loneliness

Loneliness is the deep, deserted feeling that a person experiences when he or she feels different, alone, and separate. It is an inability to be in touch with one's self—a feeling of disconnectedness. Sometimes, the deeper the loneliness, the more intense the sadness, unhappiness, and desire to find some connection with life or with oneself. Loneliness, said a little Filipino girl, is "a bear with no friends."

Rosario, a 10-year-old girl from the Philippines, had been sent to the Center with a note from her classroom teacher labeling her as "NEP" (non-English proficient). In the Philippines it is culturally correct to be reserved, unassuming, and even shy before strangers. There is an expression for this, *Na ka ka hiya:* "It is shameful." A smile or a look is a sufficient response to a stranger. Words are unnecessary. When a child is feeling *hiya*, she is silent and may respond with "I don't know" if she does not want to talk or if she is feeling "ashamed" or embarrassed to talk. This child's unresponsiveness, however, had led the teacher to think that she did not speak English at all.

I smiled at the little girl as we sat together. I spoke softly so as not to frighten her any more. I asked what province she was from, what school, and what kind of life she had had in the Philippines. I spoke some words in Tagalog, but mostly in English. She responded almost inaudibly with downcast eyes. Her silence reminded me of my own immigrant childhood days when my classmates bombarded me with questions.

How true it is, I thought, that some teachers rely too much on observations that compare immigrant children's language skills with those of others the same age, disregarding cultural backgrounds. Rosario did speak some English but preferred to be silent. To some teachers, the immigrant child may appear dysfunctional, uncooperative, unwilling, or even "dumb." But immigrant children are completely communicative in their own languages and have rich inner lives that we can ultimately reach. If we can see their inner worlds, we discover a wealth of information about what the child's experience has been and what his or her needs are.

Our simple exchange gave me a clue about where to begin with Rosario. She spoke some English and could read enough to understand. I would begin there and move her along in the same way I had with Qiu Liang. Unfortunately, neither she nor I had a say in the length of time she was to spend at the Center. Her homeroom teacher had limited her time to one period a day. She was to come in with a group of eight others and return to class with them so that "she would not miss her regular lessons and not keep up with the class." Teachers have different teaching styles, and at that time I respected her teacher's decision; but today I would probably try to keep a student like Rosario for more than one period.

At the Center, Rosario was passive and uncommunicative with the other children and appeared unmotivated to read or write. She fulfilled minimum assignments. Something troubled her, but when asked, she would clam up and say, "I don't know." Perhaps, to this polite and modest child, this meant "I don't want to say" for fear of being judged; perhaps she was not yet ready to express what she felt.

When Rosario finished reading with the group, she sat quietly preparing her lesson, her eyes often focused on the filmstrip corner of the room. She joined the group to view the stories every time a new story was presented. Then she returned to her own task. After a year of listening to the stories prepared by the other children, Rosario drummed up enough courage to write one herself. She finally risked revealing to us what was in her inner world.

One day I saw her leave her seat, and out of the corner of my eye I watched her go to the rug area. She sat in a corner for the hour and again sat there the next day with no one around her but the tape recorder and the music she had selected. She spoke quietly into the microphone until her story was complete. Unlike the others, she did not follow the process of filmstrip-making whereby all the children wrote their stories first and then made a tape. Instead, she reversed the process—first she made the filmstrip, then we wrote the story from her taped narration. Finally, when the story was complete, she beckoned me to come and view the film with her.

Our initial encounter had been one of quiet conversation in which I asked questions about her outer life; now she was presenting me with her inner world. There were no sound effects (Rosario was not yet ready to share her world with the other children); just soft melancholy music to accompany the story. We watched the film together, and I heard the tearful sadness in her voice as she spoke of a lonely bear in the woods.

■ **The Lonely Bear**

START

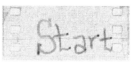

The Lonely Bear

One day, there was a bear.

He was so lonely, because he did not have any friends to play with.

So, he decided to take a walk.

When he was walking, he heard something. So [he] went to find out what it was.

And then he saw something tiny. A little squirrel was lying on the ground.

The little squirrel was hurt. He had fallen off the tree.

The bear picked it up and took it home.

He took care of it day . . .

and night.

When morning came, the little squirrel was running around the cave.

When the bear woke up, he was happy that the little squirrel was feeling better.

But soon the bear was feeling sad because he thought that the little squirrel was going to leave him.

The little squirrel went to the bear and thanked him.

And the little squirrel went out . . .

and ran to call his friends.

They followed him.

He wanted them to meet his new friend,

the bear. And they all became friends.

The End.

I sat with Rosario and felt her loneliness. I was moved by the bear's sensitivity toward the wounded squirrel, its nurturing qualities, the fear of losing friendship, and the beautiful relationship between the bear and the squirrel. From the tone of her voice I could tell that the happy ending was wish fulfillment. The warmth of this shared experience was abruptly cut off by the bell ringing. Rosario went to her next class, following the rigid schedule that can make objects of us all.

The next day I viewed the story again with her and applauded the ending. I congratulated her for a well-written story. I thought at that time that hers was a passing loneliness—one that hits all of us from time to time. I let it go at that.

Rosario taught me that the silent stage may manifest itself literally and outwardly not only by actual silence (as in the case of Qiu Liang, who couldn't speak English) but also by taciturnity (as in the case of Rosario, who *could* speak English). Her silence was kept within, held in check for years by her fear and loneliness, not detectable by teachers. For Rosario the uprooting phenomenon turned out to be more complete and lasting than I realized at the time.

Cultural Differences

At the Center I worked with a boy from Samoa who had a problem with class attendance. Before I go into his story, I want to give some background.

The children from Samoa at the school and at the Center presented a challenge because they reflected their families' difficulties with immigration: frustration, anger, and the need for survival. Samoans may come from large families, but often in our area divorce split many of the families, so the girls stayed with their mothers and the boys with their fathers in cramped home situations.

Although children from American Samoa came to the United States mainland with a command of English, most of them needed cultural validation for academic success. The school made attempts to address this situation by bringing in Samoan speakers from time to time and purchasing film stories about Samoa, but this wasn't sufficient support. Many of the children continued to challenge the teachers. Their defiance seemed to mirror the difficult situation at home, conflicts at school, and their need for attention. Their troubles were compounded when teachers would call home to report problems. The teachers were caught in a double bind because they feared their communication with the parents would result in severe punitive consequences for the child. But if they didn't call home, the children would be given the freedom to add to the already conflict-ridden multiracial situation in the schoolyard and sometimes in the classroom.

On one occasion when a teacher called home, a Samoan boy's father threw him out of the house because he had shamed the family by his actions at school. Eventually he returned home, but the teacher was upset by the result of her call. I once called home to seek support from the parents of a rebellious Samoan girl, but I later discovered to my horror that for punishment the father had cut off an inch of her hair.

However, I continued to contact parents of children other than the Samoans when necessary. Then, gradually and with great care, I began to speak to the Samoan parents in such a way that they knew I had the child's best interests in mind. I did not want the Samoan children to get the idea that home contact was out of the question—or on the other hand, that I was afraid of or intimidated by unruly behavior.

Later, in talking with cultural anthropologist Dr. Judith Barker of the University of San Francisco, I learned a lot about Samoan culture. She said:

> Throwing a child out of the house is not as serious to Samoans as to Americans, because unlike the nuclear families in the United States, Samoans have large, extended families, and there are always some next-of-kin nearby, even here in the United States. For a child to be sent out of the house provides a cooling off period for the parents and lets the child avoid constant nagging—the message merely means that it is not a good idea to be around this set of adults for a while. There is no shame, no stigma, for the child to have to move in with an aunt or uncle because in the Samoan extended family culture, the children have lots of mothers and fathers. Children are free and actually do move around to different households and still feel loved by their parents.
>
> (Barker, 1993)

Oddly enough, teachers who are appalled at a Samoan child's being thrown out of the house can, with some degree of reflection, see that they too engage in similar behavior, but the outcomes are different. A disruptive child is often removed from the classroom to cool off, sent to the principal's office, or even suspended for a few days for a serious offense. The difference between the Samoan situation and the school situation is that in the former, the child still feels loved; in the latter, the child feels unloved. When this removal is not done carefully, it backfires and the child, feeling unloved, acts out even more.

As I became more familiar with the Samoan culture, I became

aware that the Samoan church played an important role for many
Samoans. The church was the center of their lives. Barker (1993) adds
that the Samoan church is a stabilizing force for social and political
activity and the pastor is the central leader-chief and spiritual father
for the group.

I observed that, at church, the notorious children from the
schoolyard, viewing the pastor as their guide and his words as their
inspiration, often became polite and respectful.

F'aatui was a boy from American Samoa who had been more
exposed to Western culture than many of the other Samoan students.
He was 10 years old with a mischievous look about him. He was sent
to the Center to strengthen his language skills, although I suspected
he was there mostly because of his disruptive behavior in class. He
was the despair of his teacher, and soon he was to be mine. He attended school until the lunch hour, went home for lunch, and didn't
return until the next morning.

I learned from my conversation with Barker the importance of
storytelling in the Samoan culture. One of their ways "of accumulat-
ing information is through stories told to them by their elders. . . .
Samoan elders are renowned for their storytelling, which is a valued
skill in Samoa" (Barker, 1993). I wondered if in our teaching we had
lost the art of storytelling. Perhaps learning from the Samoans could
help our teaching to become more alive. The children from Samoa
were trying to tell us teachers something. I was intent on finding out.

So what would I do about F'aatui's habit of going home for lunch
each day and not returning to school? Would I be able to outsmart
him and find a creative way to get him back? If I showed him that I
was willing to meet him on his own ground while still teaching him,
might it be possible to discover what was most valuable to him?
Finally, what lessons in patience and cultural differences would I
learn from this fellow?

I began with the usual preliminary conversations that would
help me diagnose his situation. Then we set up a plan. The assignments were clear and concise; and I spoke with him firmly to indicate
that I was sure of my own authority. I felt in charge but was careful
not to be authoritarian, for that stance would awaken his defiant and
rebellious nature. I surmised that a 10-year-old feels safer if he knows
his limits and others' expectations. These limits I set for him.

Samoan boys from age 10 onward begin the cultural process of
not bending to the authority of women, says Barker (1993). The father
was the one who had to act as a mediator between F'aatui and me.
F'aatui's father worked at a gas station near the school, and I stopped
there on my way home. I asked him to intervene because the boy was
acting out and wasting his time in school. The father listened to what
I had to say and promised to speak to F'aatui. With the father's help,

F'aatui began to take school more seriously, and I continued to keep in touch with the father and report F'aatui's progress.

Next, my inquisitive mind led me to the school's filmstrip library, where I found a history of Samoa for children, complete with tapes of Samoan music. I read and listened to the tapes to see what I could learn. This filmstrip made me aware that Samoans were in touch with their instincts, which was positive. Some of the homes depicted in the filmstrip had large, open windows so the wind could bring relief from the tropical heat. There were beautiful ocean scenes. As I watched the filmstrip, I began to recall my island days and to imagine what life in Samoa was like. I closed my eyes and felt my own island soul re-awakening. I could hear the ocean, feel the warm winds, and recapture a sense of freedom and expansiveness. With that imaginary "visit" and added reading, I began to understand the boy. I also went in search for what else gave his people meaning.

For the Samoans in our area, the church provided a gathering place to sing as well as a feeling of belonging. I was touched by the amount of music and dance within the Samoan culture. Lacking a feeling of belonging in the school and without the opportunity to express themselves in music and dance, it is no wonder the Samoan children scoffed at desks as "soulless." Yet adult Samoans valued school, as evidenced by their children showing up every day and by F'aatui's father's cooperation. The families always responded when teachers called home, even if their response sometimes was too punitive from our point of view.

My plan for F'aatui unfolded as I came to understand him better— his culture and the amount of space he needed. A desk was too limiting for him. I found that most Samoan children work better as a cooperative group. I noticed that generally they would much rather all sit together and talk out issues than sit alone and read or work quietly, that they are a group-oriented people—collaborative learners. F'aatui had been lifted from his island culture and transplanted into a new milieu; my task was to guide him to integrate both worlds, to let him know I was aware of his presence in my classroom. He needed to learn to share and respect the space provided for all of us. If a teacher singles out a Samoan child (especially a boy) in a way that makes him feel guilt or shame, his or her actions will backfire, because when a Samoan child experiences extreme shame he becomes silent, stares blankly, and turns mute. This is what the Samoans call *musu*, says Barker (1993). I learned this from experience.

The rug was a comfortable place to begin with F'aatui. He seemed at home on it. I gave him the Samoan filmstrip and cassette tape, and he set it up, complete with earphones so as not to disturb the others. He was not long into the film when he spontaneously removed his earphones and with great exuberance called out, "That's

Samoa! That's Samoa!" His eyes were full of life; his body moved to the music. He viewed the film several times during that class period. I smiled at him as I was beginning to discover what he valued and what was meaningful to him.

I extracted the music from the cassette story tape and dubbed it onto another tape with F'aatui's name on it. My next plan was to use this music as background for a filmstrip story I would assign him to write. This was one time when I made the decision about when the child should make a filmstrip, because F'aatui seemed to need direction about what to do next. I showed him how to make a filmstory and asked Qiu Liang, now the "expert" and "older one," to guide him.

F'aatui's story revealed to me his need to tell the world who he was, where he came from, his name (which appeared in several frames), and where he lived. The group applauded and enjoyed seeing his filmstrip. F'aatui enjoyed it even more. Each day as he entered the room he asked to see his filmstory before beginning work. He never tired of it. "Can I see my story?" was his daily greeting.

F'aatui was so intent when watching his film that I thought he only came to class in order to see it. I seized this opportunity. The "trickster" within impelled me to say he could watch his story after lunch, for we "needed to finish the work of the morning." I said it with the same air of authority in my voice that he respected. He started to come back in the afternoon.

F'aatui was now at the Center for two periods a day. During the first period I set the assignments; during the second period after lunch, he watched his film and planned his time. Because most of his time was spent at the art table, I surrounded it with "how-to" books. In order to make boats, cars, and airplanes, F'aatui had to read. He read, he painted, he drew. He also appropriated the entire space of the long bulletin board for his own drawings. He painted and stapled until he filled the whole board. He was quiet about stapling each day, but he made his presence felt through his artwork. I did not let him see how pleased I was by his transparent and loving personality.

Once he pushed his boundaries too far and tried to get more attention than was necessary. Banging on the stapler, he glanced at me and our eyes met. That was sufficient communication between us for him to resume his quiet work.

I had worked with F'aatui only six months when he asked to talk to me. We sat at the table together, and he said he wanted to return to his regular classroom on a full-time basis. I agreed he had developed some academic skills and his behavior had improved considerably. I respected his decision to leave the Center. I felt he showed wisdom because he was being true to his cultural upbringing in that Samoans often go to an experience, learn as much as they want, and then go on to the next experience (Barker, 1993). I informed his homeroom

teacher of our work together, his need for his own space, and his
success with the filmstrip making. The teacher, in turn, made an
attempt to provide some sense of continuity between the work he did
in my classroom and the regular curriculum. She gave him the space
he needed and allowed him to continue to read the books he had been
reading at the Center.

A few days later I passed by his classroom. Out of the corner of
my eye I saw someone wave frantically. There was F'aatui, sitting at
his own desk in a special space in the back of the room with the
filmstrip projector next to him. Our eyes met. We exchanged smiles as
he pointed at the projector. I nodded with recognition. Later his
teacher told me that he had become the class expert in filmstrip
storytelling.

For F'aatui, the integration of both his worlds began when he
developed the skill of storytelling, which was valued in his culture. As
a result he asserted himself in discussions and became the "elder"
storyteller of his class.

The Child's Struggle in School

Children have innate wisdom. They often let us know what they
need—if we could only listen and hear what they are saying by their
words, artwork, and behavior.

If one believes in quick assimilation rather than acculturation,
the transplant inevitably manifests itself as a struggle within the
child. Many children have described feelings of being rushed, particularly in academic matters.

> I was always being pushed to adapt to be American. Do this and
> do that. While I was trying to adapt to one stage, it's time to
> move on to the next, and I was falling behind. It's hard—it's like
> fast-forward and you're in slow motion. Somebody was trying to
> fast-forward me.
>
> DUNG (PRONOUNCED "YOONG"),
> A GIRL FROM VIETNAM, AGE 10½

When Dung first came to the Center she was 10 years old, with
very little trace of a Vietnamese accent. She seemed extroverted,
articulate, and independent, but she was sent to me to polish her
reading skills. She was fascinated by writing filmstories and learned
the process quickly. She didn't want any help. She always seemed to
move quickly and never wanted to slow down or take time to do
anything carefully. Whatever the work, she did it, that's it, move on—
that was Dung's pattern. She gave me the impression of a restless,

extroverted person who seemed to be identified with an American persona that didn't fit her Vietnamese background. Yet on her deepest level she longed to get in touch with her Vietnamese roots, as she later expressed through her filmstrip stories.

Dung wrote her story quickly. She complained that the drawings took too much time and were a waste of time, but she completed the task. When she went to pick out her music, she was so impatient she dropped the needle onto the old records and scratched them. "Hurry, hurry," was her behavior. I decided to slow her down a bit by placing the needle on each different selection. She listened, said, "No"; listened, said, "No"; until at last she said, "That one." I watched her face light up as something in the selection seemed to touch her deeply. When I looked at the title I was amazed at her intuitiveness, because the music was called "The Dove" and her story was about a little bird—a perfect match.

The Little Egg

START

The Little Egg

One day in a little town in America, there was an egg sitting in a nest on a branch of a tree.

It just sat there all winter,

all spring,

all summer,

and all fall.

When the next year came, it still sat there all winter again.

In the spring, it hatched into a beautiful bird. .

It started to fly around the tree.

Soon, it began to fly farther away from the nest.

It flew and it flew and it flew to Vietnam.

It landed on the window of a house ...

that belonged to a little girl.

The little girl's name was Tai-Hing.

In the morning, she looked out the window and saw a tired-out little bird.

She picked it up slowly and gently and brought it to her room.

She cared for it, fed it, and kept it warm.

The bird began flying all around the house.

The bird grew bigger and bigger . . .

and soon it was time to let it go. She put it on the open window and the bird flew away.

Soon, the bird found a mate,

and they made a big nest.

The two birds came to visit Tai-Hing every year. She was expecting them every year.

The End.

Dung speaks of the transplant from one culture to another through the symbolism of an egg incubating in a nest before it is able to "hatch" into a new cultural environment. Her perceptiveness about the time it takes for an "egg" to hatch is expressed by the two winters and two springs before the egg turns into a beautiful bird. Dung is aware of the silent stage. She states clearly that without rushing the process, a child needs to feel safe until she is ready to come forth expressively—"Please do not fast-forward me." The two winters and two springs are waiting periods, and patience from the adults around her is what she needs. The newly hatched bird must fly around near the nest, building up courage and confidence, before it can venture into the unknown and build its own nest.

Dung's imagery dealt with the importance of cultural identity. Although her Vietnamese self was hidden from outsiders, her need to connect with Vietnamese roots was clearly shown in the film, because Vietnam was where the bird flew after gaining strength. The bird was her spirit. Vietnam was still important to her, still a living experience. She needed wings to get back to Vietnam, where her development began. She was seeking help to integrate both worlds. The bird in the story was also a symbol of freedom, the freedom to be herself.

While Dung was writing her story, I asked her who Tai-Hing was. She said Tai-Hing had been her teacher in Vietnam. Dung seemed to be seeking a nurturing, understanding teacher who could help her develop cognitive-academic skills like the ones she had acquired in her former culture. She spoke of Tai-Hing caring for the bird and keeping it warm. As I looked at her story, it seemed that it was after getting back in contact with the security of the "known" that the bird grew "bigger and bigger" until it was ready to seek a mate and build its own nest.

Dung presented her filmstory to the group. It was well received and the children from time to time asked to see it again.

Through her filmstrip, Dung showed me the immigrant child's need for "nesting" during the initial stages of acculturation. Children see the world both figuratively and literally; and sometimes, because they have been uprooted, they think their beliefs and values are literally "thrown to the wind" when they encounter the new culture. The "nest" provides them with a shelter where their values and beliefs can come out in the open without being ridiculed. They are free to feel different, be different, and make friends who are different. Together the children find they have more in common than they imagine.

Filmstrip-making provided the dual opportunity for children to be introverted and hide behind a tape dialogue and yet allow others to see them through the images and worlds they created. With respect for each individual's story came a respect for the child's roots.

Children from other classrooms wanted to see the filmstrip stories. I discussed this with the immigrant children, and we decided to invite an entire sixth grade class to view the films. I requested that the teacher prepare the visitors so they would be supportive and encouraging, rather than critical.

The immigrant children were enthusiastic and prepared for the big day. The room was put in order, the filmstrips were spliced together. Then we made our presentation. The visitors applauded loudly and enthusiastically, showing genuine interest, especially in Dung's story. But, to my horror, Dung hid herself under the teacher's desk in embarrassment. The "bird" had returned to its "nest." Nothing I could do or say convinced her that she had told a beautiful story. She didn't think that the "mainstream" children valued her Vietnamese tale.

I had believed Dung was ready to share her story, because in her outgoing persona she was open and confident and seemed willing to share. But sometimes an immigrant child may agree with the teacher when actually he or she feels too shy to express unreadiness to share inner thoughts and feelings with the others. In Dung's case, both of us were unprepared for her reaction. At a deep level she was Vietnamese and not ready "to express all." Although she spent most of her day in the mainstream, she kept her original culture hidden from her classmates. She was American on the outside, but Vietnamese on the inside.

Dung continued to make other filmstrips that she shared with us at the Center with themes of friendship and cultural differences. She was perceptive, wise, and talented. She knew that at the Center we understood and respected her inner self, the messages she conveyed, and the phenomenon of her uprooting.

Summary

In working with all the immigrant children at the Center, I included some of the methods I first used with Qiu Liang when time permitted. I suggest the following ways of working with immigrant children:

Acknowledge who they are—children in transition, with unique personalities and cultural histories.
Use anthropological research, books, and other sources to learn about a child's native country.
Don't be afraid to confront a discipline problem, and don't be afraid of schoolchildren who have been disruptive—but remain sensitive regarding the results of home visits.
Be an ally for the children, but don't allow them to walk all over you.
Meet the children on their own ground, in terms of their own culture, music, and history; and find a way for them to bring out their cultures' strengths.

Show them how to participate in the new society without losing important cultural values.

Show them how to make films and allow them to make these themselves.

Bring out the children's inner world through filmstrip story-telling, art, and personal experiences so as to bring their two cultures together.

Respect and trust their decisions when it is clear that they are speaking from wisdom.

Include the parents in the education and acculturation process.

Give the children a feeling of security and being grounded.

Give each child much attention without excluding the others.

Respect their "tiredness" and be aware that they are not taking advantage by being tired.

Try to investigate each situation as early as possible.

Use "how-to" books for children who are interested in making things, rather than having them sit and read any book.

Maintain continuity between your own classroom and the home-room.

Like the children.

3

Entering the
Inner World of the
Immigrant Child

Go to the people. Learn from them, live with them. Love them.
Start with what they know. Build with what they have. The
best of leaders are those when the job is done, when the task is
accomplished, the people will say, "We have done it ourselves."

LAO TSU, 604 B.C.E.

If a child is to live freely and creatively and acculturate to a new social environment, then the deeper part of the child must surface. We need to help the child remove his or her mask through warmth, reverence, understanding, and listening closely. In this chapter the children, now older, tell their stories in their own words through a process of *dual dialogic retrospection*, which is discussed later in this chapter (see page 72). Their stories help us understand the inner world of immigrant children, so that we can design programs to help them feel a sense of their own power and develop their talents to the fullest potential.

Dialogues with the Children Four Years Later

Four years had gone by since my work with the immigrant children at the Center. The images in their filmstrips—a vulnerable little egg, the staring yellow eyes of a tiger, a lonely bear, an upside-down world—haunted me, reminding me of my own uprooting experience. If their overwhelming emotions could in some way be identified and named, would it assist teachers in helping the children find their way?

When I had first developed the idea of encouraging the children to create filmstrip stories, it was with the purpose of helping them get over their shyness by allowing them to hide behind the "screen" of the filmstrips in order to speak out. This technique was meant to be used with the more introverted students, but it worked with the extroverted ones as well. At first I saw the children's stories as merely imaginative tales, but later I realized how powerfully they expressed the children's deepest feelings and thoughts. The children were the protagonists of their filmstrip stories; they were making statements in an attempt to resolve conflicts, searching for identity and taking stands.

Two boys from the Philippines had written filmstrip stories about racial conflicts and gang wars. "We do not like violence," they said. Here in the filmstrips they could speak out. One boy from El Salvador showed he was caught up in conflicts both in the schoolyard and within himself by writing about bandits robbing banks, shooting, and escaping in trains. His story revealed a boy just entering adolescence in conflict with himself. I was concerned about this message. One year later the boy acted out his filmstrip story, defying adults by wildly spray-painting the school walls. His parents became greatly concerned and sent him back to his homeland so the extended family could help him channel his energies. I would have liked to have had him interpret his filmstrip in order to gain insight into what caused the conflict. Fortunately, however, he had an extended family to guide him.

One boy from Guam had written about his country, nothing except Guam, Guam, Guam. Not until he had exhausted his need to talk about his homeland did he go on to another topic—sports. He had been able to express how frightened he felt by being in the United States because it was so large and expansive—"one could get lost if you wander too far," he wrote. In Guam he could go all around the island and always find his way back home. After he expressed all he wanted to about his homeland, he settled down and became easy to teach. He was like other children I worked with, who began to give up their "statement haircuts" and loud, disruptive behavior and started to work. I worked with this student during summer school, and he always stayed to finish his work an extra half hour or so after school. In the fall he went back to his regular "mainstream" classroom, and his troubles returned because in that classroom he felt discounted and discredited. Nothing that was important to him was included in the curriculum. No one seemed to care about Guam.

A boy from Mexico had written an interesting story about the confusion of being in a world where everything was turned around—clocks, birds, cars, even his name. Throughout the filmstrip he wrote his name several times until it was finally turned right side up. The final frame revealed a boy jumping with glee. How important it was for him to take charge of his life, to honor his name, and to reveal it to the world.

I thought about these children when I went in search of them. As part of my doctoral dissertation at the University of San Francisco, I reacquainted myself with my former students who were now on the verge of adulthood. Five of them were available to delve deeper into their immigrant experience. The dialogues with these individuals and the messages in the images left on the filmstrips of the other children cut across all cultures. I began to formulate a psychology, a philosophy; a way of thinking about children so that I could develop an environment to teach the whole child—inclusive of the child's culture.

Dual Dialogic Retrospection

> To speak means to speak to someone. . . . Hence, when a dialogue has succeeded, one is subsequently fulfilled by it, as we say. The play of statement and counter statement is played further in the inner dialogue of the soul with itself, as Plato so beautifully called thought.
>
> (Gadamer, 1976, pp. 65–66)

The methodology I used was based on principles stated by Freire (1984), who proposes that research should be a form of giving voice to the voiceless, acknowledging human beings as capable of knowing. The participatory research approach engages the participants in personal ownership and consciously draws them into interpretation. For Freire, the people who in other types of studies would be considered objects of investigation participate actively in the exploration of the themes that emerge in their lives so that they can participate in their own transformation. The investigation, he says, is one of humanization rather than of reducing people to things; the investigator needs to be someone who does not fear change, because rigidity is a "killer of life."

The methodology for my research was also based on Kieffer's (1981) dialogic retrospection, wherein the participants are involved as collaborators in the research process as they reflect on their experience. In this process, the participants are engaged in personally meaningful critical reflections on their own individual growth experiences. The subjects become active partners throughout the research process as they generate data and interpret it. The participatory approach is different from the traditional research model, which implies researcher control of investigative process and outcomes. In participatory research the actions are not imposed from above but come from within the individuals themselves.

When I reconnected with the children, I expanded Kieffer's methodology. I call the methodology I used in my contact with the five students *dual dialogic retrospection* (Igoa, 1988). The research was unique in that both student and teacher reflected on the same experience at the Center. Where students had forgotten incidents, I could recall them; and the students, in turn, could recall incidents I had forgotten. As a result, it became a learning process for the students and myself; both have been changed by the experience and dialogue—a new awareness has developed. The research was also unique in that the students' voices had been preserved on tape, as well as the images and messages on the filmstrips. This facilitated the students' reflections.

At times it is difficult to do research with children because they may be apt to say what adults want to hear, or they may say "I don't know" when they are afraid or do not wish to reveal their feelings and thoughts. In this study, the children were on the verge of adulthood and therefore less inhibited as they reflected on their childhood experience. The tapes and filmstrips contained their feelings and thoughts— waiting for their recollections and interpretations to give a fuller picture of themselves.

To engage in dialogue, says Freire (1984), is to communicate with commitment and to devote oneself to the constant transformation of reality in the loving encounter of people. This encounter humanizes the world.

There is an important difference between an *interview* and the *process of dialogue*. The meeting with my former students was not the occasion for an interview. In an interview, one is the giver of information and the other, the receiver; the giver may begin to feel that he or she is the "object" of study. Being an object dehumanizes the person. In a dialogue, one or the other may become intent on making a point, and that may lead to an argument. However, a change can occur in both participants if each has respect for the language and personality of the other.

The introvert reflects and then speaks; the extrovert thinks while speaking. In a dialogue, sufficient time is crucial. There needs to be time for one person to listen to what the other is saying, time to clarify words, time to, hear what is being said, and time for both persons to feel heard and understood. They are then changed by the experience. In a genuine dialogue, each party respects the freedom to leave unspoken what he or she has in mind. Each allows for reflection about what has been spoken in order to comprehend fully the new insights gained.

In our encounters with other humans we often forget the concept of dialogue. We do not listen to what is behind the words or ask for clarification before we draw conclusions. Misunderstandings occur in human relationships when we fail to communicate clearly or when one person is caught up in exercising power. "I am right. You are wrong." Yet if we were to stop and ask what the other means by these words, a simple rephrasing might indicate an altogether different meaning. What is said and what is meant can then be sorted out by the one speaking and the one listening. Transformation can take place.

Even when people come from the same culture, entanglements and misunderstandings can happen. When they come from two different cultural backgrounds, interpretations can vary even more. Meanings can be lost in translation; the speaker can be confused by the expectations, experiences, and projections of the listener. Misconceptions can result. In my dialogue with the students I was very careful to listen and ask for clarification, because I wanted to arrive at their truths and learn their experiences with no judgment or preconceptions. In the dialogue I shared my perceptions of our time at the Center when they were applicable, so the students would feel I was walking with them. Together we would reflect and share equally, fostering trust in the bond that had been established at the Center.

Consulting with other professionals (as I had done with Dr. Barker, the anthropologist, about F'aatui) has been part of my teaching style. It enlarges my perspective when teaching children from many different cultures. Because I wanted to formulate a psychology of working with immigrant children, I decided to confer with two psychologists (Dr. George Wilson and Florence Grossenbacher, M.A.) for interpretations of the filmstrips other than those provided by the children. Both psychologists worked with me under the direction of Dr. Brian Gerard of the Education and Counseling Psychology Department at the University of San Francisco. I have included in footnotes or in the text itself minimal information from these consultations that might be useful for teachers. At all times, however, we all agreed that the children's own interpretations had the greater authority.

Themes from the Dialogues

The Voices of the Children

Qiu Liang Speaks

I was eager to meet Qiu Liang (Dennis) again. I had not seen or heard of him since his profound message: "Dennis is alive." He was now in his last year of high school. We had established a close relationship during our two years at the Center and I had become very fond of him. As I waited for him to come down from class, I wondered what he would be like. In just a few minutes Qiu Liang, much taller now, stood by the counselor's office door with a questioning look as he focused his attention on the counselor. "I have someone here who wants to see you. Do you recognize her?" she asked. Qiu Liang paused as he looked toward me and then he exclaimed, "Oh!" With arms outstretched he reached out. There was real joy at that meeting.

Qiu Liang was very much at ease. His eyes were penetratingly sincere; he had a smile on his face. He sat in the counselor's chair. The counselor had now left us to ourselves. After a brief silence, he gestured, "What's up?" It had been a while since our last communication. Where would I begin?

I spoke hesitatingly, with the same caution I had when Qiu Liang was a child, about my desire to understand the immigrant experience and how I needed students to participate in a study. "You can ask me anything," he said reassuringly. "I speak very well now."

There had been a time when I reassured him. Now he was reassuring me, his countenance calm. We spoke of the time we had spent at the Center and of his high school years. "They put me in ESL classes that were so easy, but I didn't say anything," was his recollection.

We made plans to engage in dialogue from time to time over a couple of years to see what direction his life would take and what insights into himself he could provide. He was enthusiastic and accommodating. But before we parted, I asked the question I had been burning to understand: What was the reason for his long silence and the fear he showed in the filmstrips? Qiu Liang responded without hesitation, having been familiar with his inner world long enough to know:

> *Back in China all the people are just the same kind. . . . At first (in America) I was so scared. I locked myself in my room and wanted to remain close to my family. I was afraid to leave them. I locked myself in for a week, but my father made me go to school.*

Much of Qiu Liang's fear was related to the strangeness of the people he encountered: Anglo, African American, Hispanic, and other Asians all mixed together. His reaction to his fear was to isolate himself literally and figuratively from others. I understood his old fear well, as I recalled my own experiences in China (the China from which Qiu Liang was uprooted). During my visit at the end of the Cultural Revolution, when the Bamboo Curtain of Communism had just opened and Western visitors could enter only with government permission, I was with a group and at all times with a government guide. In Chapter 2 I describe my visit to a Chinese school while I was on this trip. Here, I want to describe one occasion when I managed to slip away to a back street where Western feet had not trod in more than twenty years. Fascinated by the patterns of a hand-woven rug on the outside of a store, I lifted my camera to snap a picture.

From all around me searching Chinese eyes stared. Within that split second between curiosity and action, I had become surrounded by hundreds of staring eyes. No one made a sound; their faces were totally serious and indicated the once forbidden nature of a smile. I was a "giant" in flashing pink and white. They were in uniform blue with regulation hair styles.

That universal fear of the unknown grabbed me. In the seeming seriousness of the moment and surrounded by the crowd, I imagined that the people were angry at my intrusion. I quietly put the camera away and hastened back to my group. Later I was told by a Chinese man not to mistake their serious looks. The crowd wasn't angry, but inquisitive. They were fascinated by the camera, my pink and white outfit, and my height—they meant well.

That experience helped me to understand Qiu Liang. If I had been so afraid in China, how much more fearful had he been in his new country? I was an adult; he, a child.

As my dialogues with Qiu Liang continued, he graduated from high school, went to college, and had an after-school job teaching Chinese children in Chinatown. He explained that his family had left China for political reasons and had traveled briefly to Hong Kong before coming to the United States. Although he had begun to study English in Hong Kong, the difference between the alphabet system and Chinese characters made learning English difficult. "It was hard to learn English in Hong Kong because I hardly knew how to write A, B, C."

Resistance to change.   Qiu Liang spoke of his resistance to the change:

I didn't want to change 'cause I was used to the kind of life I was living in China. But I changed to a new environment. It was different for me because it upset the kind of life I had.

Qiu Liang recalled with pleasure the time we spent at the Center. He had not forgotten making the filmstrips. Several times he reviewed the filmstrips he had made and remarked:

> *I liked doing the filmstrip story, saying feelings. It was not just the gingerbread boy I'm talking about, it's something related to me. At the time, I felt the same way as the gingerbread boy . . . very happy inside, but still hard for me to show up, back then, show out, you know. I felt it was hard for me to tell them all that I felt; express it, so I just kept it inside myself.*
>
> *I was beginning to open up because I knew some people in there, some friends, and I knew you better because we had been together for a month. So I began to feel like home, a place like home, almost like my home. And that's why I decided to do this filmstrip.*
>
> *The story has a happy ending. Throughout the whole film, the boy feels carefree, nothing to worry about . . . like just enjoying life, doing things, and doesn't have anything on his mind that he's worrying about.*

In my dialogues with Qiu Liang he revealed that the overall theme of the filmstrip story, *Gingerbread,* is that Qiu Liang is beginning to find things he likes to do. The gingerbread boy is very active, playing in the park, going home for lunch, opening presents, making a snowman. The filmstrip gave a whole picture of Qiu Liang. It had been a way of finding out what was going on inside him; it had been an outlet for his silent world. Once he felt sheltered and safe, he was able to express himself. What he expressed was more happiness than could be observed by looking at him.[1]

Feeling vulnerable. Qiu Liang's feelings of vulnerability were clearly depicted in the section of the filmstrip when the gingerbread boy saw a baby bird fall down. Qiu Liang commented:

> *Why the little bird fell has to do with how I felt, how other immigrant students felt—helpless, hopeless. The immigrants feel others think they can't do things.*

[1] When I discussed Qiu Liang's interpretation of his filmstrip story with Dr. George Wilson (1986, 1987), the psychologist said that Qiu Liang had picked up American images and was trying to deal with them, that he was beginning to see hope, that good things could come from this culture too. Gingerbread successfully runs away from danger. When Qiu Liang interpreted Gingerbread as a projection of himself, he identified himself as someone good and worthwhile. Gingerbread is a survivor. If Gingerbread makes it, Qiu Liang too can make it. The happy story compensates for his fears and his feeling threatened.

Qiu Liang also recalled his fear of ridicule by others as part of the reason for his silence:

> *I was afraid to say anything. I was afraid people would make*
> *fun and laugh at me because of my feeling different from others.*
> *I kept quiet.*

In fact, it was unlikely that other students singled out Qiu Liang as an oddity. It was more likely that in view of the multiethnic population of the school, the other students didn't consider him particularly unusual. Nevertheless, his feeling that they did was real enough to Qiu Liang.

Loss of native culture and language. Qiu Liang deeply felt the loss of his culture and the uselessness of his language at school. The stress of acculturation was reflected at the end of the filmstrip when the gingerbread boy went home "very tired." In the words of Qiu Liang:

> *The "very, very tired" means he [the gingerbread boy] went*
> *through a lot. That he goes through a lot that day, the whole day,*
> *and that he tries to be with the others—tries to be the same as*
> *the others . . . to blend in with the others. It is still very difficult*
> *for him to do so. After he tried for a whole day, he was tired. It*
> *was too much to handle in one day.*

As I listened to Qiu Liang interpret his filmstrip, I wondered why a child must bear the sole responsibility to blend in with the others. Why shouldn't the others come halfway and reach out to an immigrant child, who carries within him a rich history and culture?

When immigrant children identify with representations like the vulnerable baby bird, they begin to act helpless and hopeless; and when they think others see them that way, they begin to fear others' ridicule. Their creative energy becomes blocked. The task of unblocking that inquisitive, playful, imaginative force within necessitates the awakening of the teacher's own inquisitive, imaginative, and playful nature. Through the teacher's creative self, he or she can find ways to help the child.

The second filmstrip, *Near the Mountain*, written shortly after the *Gingerbread* filmstrip, is rich in symbols, meaning, and a sense of adventure as the boys go to look at, not run away from, the two yellow eyes. The yellow eyes represent the immigrant child's fear that others are "staring at him," Qiu Liang explained.

> *It was hard back then for me to go into a classroom. I was new*
> *and I felt like everybody was looking at me and staring at me.*

But I think it was only in my mind; I just thought they were. I don't think they really were doing that. When I went home, I was thinking about how those people might think of me.

In this story, the mountain represents the difficult road an immigrant child must travel. Qiu Liang said:

The mountain, I believe, is like life—not as smooth . . . you have to go through other changes and difficult times . . . ups and downs. Just like life. So you just have to get used to it and a new environment.

Fear was the most profound emotion Qiu Liang felt as a child in a new land. By the time he made this filmstrip, he was beginning to adjust to the demands of his new life—even with its difficulties. But life was still tough and dangerous because, said Qiu Liang, "The tiger is a symbol of fear, the two boys are like immigrants. The new country has a lot of changes and new people. The two boys are afraid." The boys took refuge in the home of an old couple. Qiu Liang spoke of the shelter as a refuge from the tiger. The man shot the tiger, making the mountain safe again.

The man shot the tiger—the tiger is like a fear and so now there are no more fears. [The man] is the person who helps the immigrants. The teacher—in this case it's you that helped him get through, blend into a new culture so at the end there are no more fears. They feel that they are part of a new culture. The tiger is the fear of the new country—the change, the people in the new country, the men who shot the tiger. So at the end, the fear was gone.

Need for relationship with teacher and friends. Qiu Liang spoke of the relationship between teacher and immigrant child being an important factor for helping him overcome his fear and helping him bridge the gap between cultures.[2] Qiu Liang also spoke about the critical role of friends:

Yes, friends help a lot. If you don't have friends, you just sit there quiet. You are always looking at the clock. You wonder when the time will finish. It's very hard to live like that. But if you have friends and they talk to you and you do things together, that makes a difference.

---

[2] The question for Qiu Liang, said Wilson (1987), was not "how to exist in his own house, but how to exist outside his house with new images. . . . To feel that one can have a friend is a big step to actually being able to get one."

At the Center, his classmates had collaborated with him in making the sound effects, and they as well as I had loudly applauded when the filmstrips were shown. The Center then became a "home away from home" for him. Here Qiu Liang was free from others "staring at him" and he could express himself without fear of ridicule, as no "outsiders" were allowed in the Center without invitation. It was a place of security and strength.

The feeling of security also existed because I had designed the Center in response to the children themselves, who had each expressed their criteria for a shelter either verbally or nonverbally. Qiu Liang explained:

> [In the Center] you learn more because in a regular classroom,
> it's a lot of people, it's a lot of students, so the teacher cannot
> deal with every student . . . can't sit down with that one student
> for a long period of time. With fewer students, the teacher knows
> the student better, and the students can get to know the teacher
> better.

Qiu Liang's final filmstrip still contained the elements of fear and safety that characterized his previous stories, but a new maturity was evident. His voice was strong and confident. He "felt really happy so that's why I included, 'Thank you, everybody.' " At this point he had internalized the children's applause, felt his success, and believed "other people began to notice me, and they acted interested in what I was doing." He felt recognized, he belonged, he was no longer an "outsider." He noted that "occasionally 'it' [fear] would show up again, but someone is always there to help you get through it. . . . I was not going through it by myself."

In *The Wolf*, Qiu Liang no longer asked permission "to go into a shelter" as he did in the tiger story. He shut the door on his own. He was able to keep the wolf scratching at the door outside. His fear of other people took on more realistic proportions, and he began to see that he did have friends who made him feel "happy and safe." He "began to notice that they care."

The school environment was important for a sensitive boy such as Qiu Liang. He needed his native culture and language to be valued as he adjusted to living in a new culture.[3] When I asked Qiu Liang what was going through his mind when he was writing his Chinese name, he responded:

---

[3] Wilson (1987) said: "He could have been badly hurt by the wrong environment. It was crucial for him to honor his bicultural dimension because he could have been alive yet lost his roots."

I think it was pretty fun because you're writing Chinese and the [other students] do not even know what it means, so they have to ask you what it means and you enjoy telling them that's your name in Chinese.

Integrating two cultures. It was at this crucial moment that Qiu Liang felt a sense of equality with the others. The feeling of being "different" was no longer a threat; he enjoyed being himself. Years later he still felt like a Chinese boy. "I always remind myself that I am Chinese so I won't forget." Knowing two languages, he said, one has to "think differently."

It was good to be with Qiu Liang, whose personality had expanded to integrate both his worlds. I sensed his divergent mode of thinking as we talked—his reflective thinking as he probed both sides of a question, seeing more than one way of doing things, being flexible.

Alice Speaks

When I met Alice again, we had a warm encounter. She had been the "little banana," efficient and serious, who gave in to laughter when we imitated the banana doing exercises each morning. Alice's time at the Center had been limited.

She seemed fine on the outside and devoid of inner conflict. She had learned to speak, read, and write, and she spoke English without a trace of accent. She was planning to apply to a well-known university. Her grades were excellent.

Alice, Qiu Liang's sister, had been 8 years old when she arrived in the United States and spoke no English. She recalled how helpful teachers were to her in the U.S. schools, but she also remembered the pain she experienced when "cruel students" called her names and she had to eat lunch entirely alone during her first days at school. Those unpleasant memories still stung.

Like her brother, Alice had experienced an extreme shock in moving from the Chinese to the U.S. culture, so that in almost every dimension of her life she felt a difference. She was overwhelmed at the abundance, the lack of strict government control over everything, and the differences in the school systems. In China, teachers "taught more—explaining everything very fully," rather than expecting students to learn on their own. Students worked harder in China, she observed. They listened more carefully and worked more diligently. She spoke of corporal punishment in the schools in China, the respect for teachers, and the fact that there were no report cards.

When we spoke about the filmstrip *The Little Banana*, Alice had fond memories of writing the story. She had developed a sense of humor and laughed at the banana's independent and capable nature. The happy theme indicated that she had been feeling much more comfortable with herself at the time she made the filmstrip than she had felt right after her arrival.

> *This may sound funny, but I think at the time my favorite fruit was banana. I think that's why I did it on a banana.*

When she reflected on the filmstrip and its general lightheartedness, she was surprised to see the unconscious messages of feeling good and being able to do things competently.

Loneliness.   On closer inspection, some aspects of the film showed that Alice had still suffered from loneliness. Even the topic of the banana, which reflects the close relationship between food and friends, demonstrated her initial aloneness. When I asked her to explain what it was like to be alone, silent, and unable to communicate with anyone, she responded:

> *Scary! Well, not scary, but it was just a very bad experience. There are no words to describe it.*

Alice had drawn four Xs around the banana in the filmstrip. She explained:

> *Every time he [the banana] was by himself, I put some Xs just to make it seem crowded . . . so he wasn't alone . . . a feeling of something being around him . . . not loneliness—to make it look [like] four. The banana had Xs to represent, maybe, friends around him. I wanted everyone to be around me.*

Repeatedly in my dialogues with Alice she mentioned how important a friendly gesture was to her. She admitted being lonely that first year in the United States:

> *It was just so happy for me the day I finally found a friend. A lot of people talked to me, but that was all they did . . . a girl finally was really my friend. She would eat lunch with me, do everything with me. Before, I did everything by myself. It was hard to explain. It was joy. Because there was someone there to be with, to do everything with you. It was just great.*
>   *I remember in fourth grade there was this new girl also and she was really quiet and she was from Vietnam. She's still my friend right now.*

Alice suffered many of the same experiences of aloneness and separateness as her brother Qiu Liang:

> Some of the kids called me names because I was Chinese, although there were other Chinese students there. But then they called me names and I was really mad and sad at the same time. I didn't like the fact that they treated me different, right? I was just a different nationality.
>
> It was hard for those people who called me names to know what I was feeling, because they were never discriminated [against]. You don't know how discrimination feels until you are discriminated [against]. When they called me names . . . it was anger and frustration. It was hard to understand why they were so cruel. It was easy for them to be cruel because I was the outsider and everyone else was just a group against me. I was by myself, so there was no way I could defend myself.

Silence as protection. Alice's defense was to remain silent. She guarded her feelings and was unable to express her emotions to her parents or her classmates:

> I couldn't exactly tell my parents [how I felt nor could I tell] . . . the other kids. I couldn't even communicate with them, so there was no way I could try to make things better for myself. It was hard feeling just bad.

Alice felt trapped inside a quiet, silent body when she first arrived. Her pain was evident when she said:

> I didn't participate in a lot of stuff. I wanted to. You know, the other kids were doing certain things and I looked at them. I said, "Oh, they're having fun. I want to do that." But then, I was reluctant to do that because I felt maybe I couldn't do that, right? Maybe I thought I wasn't good enough to do what they were doing. It was really bad to just sit there and look at what they were doing with the feeling that I wanted to do it but just couldn't.

Alice's reluctance to speak English was initially tied to her fear that the others would laugh at her:

> I thought if I tried to speak I would say something wrong and pronounce a word wrong. They would laugh at me, tease me, whatever. So it took me a while before I could really use the language, just speak it, but then I overcame that.

Alice's inability to communicate, her loneliness, and her feeling different made her feel "totally helpless." She felt she could do nothing, until

> *They realized I wasn't that different from them and they just stopped calling me names and I was part of the group.*

The story depicts a resolution to that pain and helplessness when the banana goes back to the apple tree to find a nourishing apple. The banana shows initiative, which helps it grow out of its helplessness.[4]

Academic problems. Alice felt extremely uncomfortable about her inability to perform in school:

> *Well, in the fourth grade, because I didn't speak English, my grades were really bad. Very bad. I mean, I was just kind of disappointed in myself because I couldn't do anything that people my age could do.*
>
> *Mostly I got Cs. The only class I got an A in was math. You know, because it's the same in the whole world. Everyone learns math; it's the same. But then English, science, and other classes, I didn't do well because I didn't speak English so I couldn't read the books. So that was really disappointing. I was afraid to make mistakes, afraid that people would laugh at me. So I didn't speak much. But eventually I overcame that. By the time I was in fifth grade, I was speaking English already and my grades improved and everything. So I was really happy. At that time I was really happy with myself.*
>
> *By the time I was in fifth grade, I was pretty good with the language already because I learned really young. Plus, I was always with friends and everything so it was really easy to learn. And by the time I was in sixth grade, everything was just normal. I didn't have any problems anymore.*

It is clear that Alice's oral language development was intimately tied to others—positively, in that talking with others helped her to develop English ability; and negatively, in that she was reluctant to speak for fear others would make fun of her. In the regular classroom, she had been working at "a lower level" than her peers, according to her teacher, and she had difficulty with written English. The Center became a safe place for her to perform at her own pace and to her own level.

---

[4] In looking over Alice's filmstrip story, Wilson (1987) commented: "The underlying personality is an autonomous individual who takes care of herself, does her routine exercises, is organized, and has a good house. The outlook for a successful life is positive. It may be lonely, but she can do it. Although she could not find people, she could nourish herself."

I think that was my favorite class. That was the only class that I could really do well in and not have to compete with other peo-ple. . . . I did everything that I could do instead of other people trying to make me do things I couldn't . . . and I was really com-fortable there. The class really helped me. Everybody else was at the same level as I was, so I wasn't scared.

Caught between two cultures.   Alice was articulate and extroverted. She spoke of her cultural conflict, of which she had not been aware, but which surfaced during our dialogues.

I see myself as somewhere in between. I'm caught in between. Because at home my parents expect me to be not a traditional Chinese daughter . . . but they expect things because I was born in China and I am Chinese. And at school, that's a totally differ-ent story because you're expected to behave as an American. You know, you speak English in your school; all your friends speak English. You try to be as much of an American as you can. So I feel I'm somewhere caught in between.

I wake up every morning and look in the mirror and think, "I have to act American." Then on my way home from school, I sit in the bus and think, "I have to act Chinese." Before this interview . . . I wasn't aware of how I was caught in between . . . I feel I can no longer be fully Chinese or fully American any-more.

Pressure to assimilate.   Somewhere in the rush to assimilate, to avoid the pain of name-calling, Alice had set aside her past so that outwardly she seemed well adapted to American society. I was con-cerned when I listened to her. How stamped she seemed in the Ameri-can pattern. Although she had lost some mastery of written Chinese, she could still converse with relatives in Hunan, Mandarin, and Can-tonese. She longed to become more bilingual, and that longing may in time move her to further integrate both worlds.

It's hard not to understand your own language . . . not to know your own language more than a second language, which is Eng-lish for me. I probably forgot over 70 percent of what I learned since first grade. . . . So I don't feel very comfortable about not knowing more Chinese than I do English.

What is significant about Alice's story is that she succeeded all throughout school with very little support. She "made it" on her own initiative, struggling through fears, discrimination, anger, and frustra-tion with only her first grade schooling in China as a foundation. The dialogues gave her a start in understanding how she was caught between two cultures.[5]

Cindy Speaks

Cindy was the child who wrote the filmstory entitled *The Upside Down Morning.* Cindy and her family were from Hong Kong on the Kowloon side. She had two years of schooling in Kowloon and was enrolled in the third grade when she came to the United States. At this time, the family changed her Chinese name (which she never revealed to me) to "Cindy." Her grandparents had immigrated twelve years earlier, and an older aunt was a U.S. citizen.

Although Cindy had spent only one hour per day at the Center, we had established a trusting relationship. Cindy had not forgotten our time together and was eager to speak about her immigrant experience. Had I been a teacher who was a total stranger, she would have not said much now, she commented.

When I saw her again she had become tall, slender, reflective, and gracious. Meeting her was a delight. At the time of our dialogues, her retired grandparents lived with Cindy's family. Her father, who had worked as a government official in Hong Kong, was working as a clothing salesman; her mother had become a cook in a fast-food restaurant. She had an older sister and a younger brother.

Struggles with a new language.   In Hong Kong, Cindy had been exposed to some British English and could understand it slightly. American English was completely incomprehensible to her. In the United States she lived in a low-income neighborhood where she had few friends who spoke Chinese—a motivating factor to speed up her learning of English. She learned to speak and understand English in one year, although it is important to understand that this does not mean cognitively demanding language or "academic" language, which requires a longer time.

She expressed her difficulty about not being able to socialize in the school:

> [*School*] *was so difficult. I mean, everybody was in on the conversation. They had class discussions and communicated with each*

[5] Wilson (1987) commented: "Seeing the example of her brother, who is comfortable both ways, will help her become more comfortable at an older age." "She guarded her feelings," said Grossenbacher (1988), "as she was caught in a double bind because of discrimination." Wilson (1987) added: "There is nothing in the outer world that says she needs to remain Chinese. That's all adaptation and blending like everyone else. Listening to her inner call would make her a real person; a more conscious human being. To be an individuated American, one needs to have a sense of history."

*other. . . . I felt alone because there weren't that many people that
could communicate with me. I was pretty quiet, I think. There was
only one student besides myself who was Chinese . . . we didn't
talk that much in the beginning . . . she's also kind of shy.*

*I think I learned English in about a year. I think I could under-
stand . . . the main reason was the people around me didn't
speak Chinese.*

Cindy enjoyed being sociable. In Hong Kong she had had many
friends; but without the ability to communicate in English, she had
only one friend in school and her family with whom she could share
experiences. This situation was too limiting for her.

Cindy experienced the initial excitement and curiosity of a child
traveling to America, but then she was unprepared to stay.

*I think that period of time gave me a feeling kind of depressed when
I realized we were not going back. Well, basically it was because I
had all my friends in Hong Kong, and we were really close. We
shared a lot of things. Since we came here, we still kept in touch
through letters and we told each other what's going on. I was
depressed at least for about a year. I just basically kept it to myself.*

Although Cindy learned to speak English quickly, it took her from
grade three to grade six or seven to feel she had "mastered the English
language." She was concerned about keeping up with the others, so
she felt she had to leave her Chinese language behind.

*[In school here] there were no special classes for Chinese . . .
[and even if there were special classes in Chinese] I don't think
it would have affected my eagerness in learning English. . . . If I
had a Chinese tutor then probably my homework time in English
would have been affected by an hour or two . . . it would take a
little time from my studying English. . . . I really wanted to learn
English at that point because everybody was communicating in
English.*

Differences between native and U.S. educational systems. Cindy felt the
difference between the two school systems. In Hong Kong she was
"basically very quiet"; in America everybody spoke what they felt.
Teachers "were a lot stricter" in Hong Kong—the environment here
was "totally different" from what she had been used to. Teachers could
hit students across the hand with a ruler if they misbehaved, whereas
in America the teachers "really reached out" and tried to help her. They
put a Chinese classmate next to her in the United States, because at
first she "didn't understand anything at all." In Hong Kong students
were ranked according to academic achievement and she was always

"right in the middle, stuck in the middle." Students in the U.S. schools changed classes; students in Hong Kong stayed in one classroom and the teachers moved. In Hong Kong "99 percent of the people were Asian"; in the United States there were many ethnic groups.

Fear and exhaustion in a strange new world. Cindy experienced an "upside-down" world, as the title of her filmstory indicated. Her story showed that dealing with all the differences was exhausting. She was "scared and ran home."

When I asked her to share some of her thoughts about the film-strip story, she said:

> *I think that home was a place where I could be by myself and not have anyone else there. Because at that age, I didn't express my feelings that much. I just liked to be by myself. So I think in the story, I was so scared I ran home. Home represented any place where I could be by myself and feel secure and safe. I think I got tired from that walk. It's like I . . . experienced so many things just by that one walk. I consumed so many different incidents that I felt really stressed out.*
>
> *I think the nap basically represented a form of escape from reality at that point. I think the upside-down world was about the stage I was in. . . . I was probably kind of confused and not sure of what was going on. And the upside-down world, every-thing's upside down and kind of mixed up . . . [I got tired] and went back to sleep. Maybe that was a way of showing what I wanted . . . hoping everything would be okay when I woke up.*

The events in Cindy's filmstrip were not bad events—just a suc-cession of events so strange that they were exhausting.

> *I think I was talking about having consumed everything and let-ting things just sit there for a while and deal with them as they come along instead of trying to think about it all at once.*

At home, Cindy's parents encouraged her to study and do well in school. She had a "safe" bedroom and went to a library when the images of the new country became too much for her.

Her peers liked her filmstrip story, which evoked laughter and acceptance. That Cindy was a creative child was clear in her colorful images.[6]

---

[6] Wilson (1987) commented: "She thinks of things as both disturbing and funny. In a stressful time of anxiety, humor is incredibly helpful. I think if I saw this filmstrip at the time the child had done it, I would say her outlook was good. An upside-down world is really an apt image. I think we need to be very aware of how a foreign culture at first puts an input overload on a person."

Even though Cindy found it alright for other students to speak in class, she herself did not participate even after she had gained fluency in English. She attributed her silence to both her own nature and her previous school experience.

> *I usually think about what I'm going to say. Still, now, when I have something to say, I think about it first; but I usually take too long because by the time I want to say it, we have already passed that point and we're moving on to the next question.*

Need for affirmation from teachers and peers. Making the filmstrip helped Cindy overcome some of her natural shyness. In thinking back about it, she recalled that she enjoyed using her imagination to make her own film. Initially when I had presented the films to visitors from one of the "mainstream" classes, Cindy said, "We were all going crazy. We would hide our faces." When their stories were shown, Cindy said, the students felt as if they were "freaking out," yet they were unable to object because as she mentioned, "having part of my education in Hong Kong, it was, whatever the teacher says, goes."

She recalled that making the film was very good for her:

> *I remember some of the kids from a different class telling me it was funny. I got positive responses to it. And I guess that's why at the end, I was glad that you did show it.*

Caught between two cultures. Our dialogues were helpful for Cindy. They clarified for her that although she was already comfortable with English, she wanted to regain fluency in her native language. She had already started speaking Chinese whenever possible at home and outside her home.

> *A couple of days ago I was thinking, I really hope to go into one of the Chinese classes during my years in college. . . . I believe that since that's my original background and that's the language of my ancestors and also my parents and relatives—most of my relatives do not speak any English at all—I think it's really important to keep the communication going . . . understand what they are trying to tell me and be able to tell them what I feel. So it's really important to keep the roots. . . . Also when we travel, I think it would be hard to communicate if I didn't know any Chinese. I am an American citizen now, but I still have that feeling, that strong feeling, that I want to know about my background.*

Cindy experienced some difficulty with cultural identity because of her dual cultural experience and language. It was hard, she said, "because at school you would speak English, but when at home I would speak Chinese." In Cindy's early enthusiasm to learn English, she began using it at home in spite of her grandfather's admonishment that the children must talk in Chinese. As she got older, she resented her great-uncle's comment that she would be "classified as someone born here" because she had arrived at such a young age.

Rosario Speaks

As a teacher–researcher, I learned from the dialogues that my former students were straightforward, open, and honest. I was aware of their sincerity and wisdom and met with them wherever quiet space was available—in a classroom, in their living rooms, at a restaurant, or wherever they suggested. I usually gave several possibilities but left the final choice of a meeting ground to them.

In the car on the way to the university library was where Rosario began her story. She had taken a job in a tourist shop. Almost immediately she related to me as if we had been best friends. Our initial dialogues began toward the end of her third year of high school and were completed two years later. Her filmstory, *The Lonely Bear*, was still vivid in my mind, and I wondered what had become of him.

Rosario had come to the United States with her family when she was 6 years old. She was the youngest of two brothers and five sisters—seven children in all. Both parents had jobs: the father with an insurance company, the mother at a hotel. During our dialogues she expressed that as a child she had had little interaction with her parents, as they were too exhausted to relate to her when they returned home from work. Nor was she close to any other member of her family, as the older siblings were too busy with school activities.

Shyness. In our dialogues Rosario was warm and friendly and only gave in to the shyness (*hiya*) when her relatives embarrassed her in front of me for not having graduated from high school. She then became reluctant to speak, answering softly, "I don't know." To get her out of feeling *hiya*, we drove around, stopped by a Filipino restaurant, and chatted. But each time we returned to the subject of school, she would withdraw into her shyness. She blamed herself for "being lazy" and skipping school. She watched television until the early hours of the morning and slept during the day.

Need for a "safe nest." At moments when she was less embarrassed, she expressed wanting to make it in school and said that a counselor had been helping her. Had he not left after Rosario's first year at the high school, she felt, she would have graduated.

Rosario's education got off to a poor start because she was moved from school to school five times on account of her lack of fluency in English. She had no recollection of attending the first grade. Her two years at the Center were uneventful, as she came for a limited time and always worked with a group. She was mainly the responsibility of her homeroom teacher. Yet her filmstrip story about a lonely bear showed that she had a lot to say about the theme of loneliness and relationships or lack of relationships, and what it meant to be alone. In our dialogues she did recall she had written a story about a bear.

Loneliness.   During the time Rosario talked with me, she watched *The Lonely Bear* several times. She did not like the story. The story was about a lonely bear, she said. The bear "had no friends and no one was around for him." It seemed to me to reflect her unresolved loneliness and her inability to integrate happily with her family and society. She commented that she liked the ending where the bear made friends.

As reflected in her filmstrip, Rosario was an introverted and lonely child when she first came to the Center. The story was a plea for help, a plea for "support from someone."

> *I was lonely and alone and sad. I wasn't sure I'd still make it in school. And I had no friends.*
> *I felt kind of odd because I didn't know anyone. There was only me and my sister. And I didn't really know anyone here. Because I didn't know anyone and I couldn't speak English . . . that well. I just came from the Philippines. It was hard for me to communicate with other people.*

Her current reserve and her aloneness seemed to be an extension of the loneliness she had felt as an immigrant child.

> *I just like to spend time by myself sometimes. I just go off and listen to the radio. I watch TV . . . sometimes I go out with my friends . . . but most of the time I like to be alone. I hardly stay home that much because I'm always out. I don't really get along with my sisters that much.*

Need to feel understood.   Rosario felt she had always been alone, silent, and wrapped up in herself—that no one really understood her. She had felt this way "for as long as I can remember."

> *Sometimes they understand me; but sometimes they can't really understand the way I am.*

Unfortunately, Rosario was not able to find understanding in the Center. She did not establish a relationship with me or with the other children. This may have been because of the relatively little amount of contact I had with her—only one period per day for two years, the large reading group, and the number of students in her regular class. No one really got to know her personally. But in our dialogues now that Rosario was older, we were able to share experiences in which I came across as a friend and not as a teacher.

When reflecting on her filmstrip, Rosario acknowledged that the bear was herself. The pictures showed the many sides of the bear. He was alone, in tears, and nurturing a squirrel. Her wish was for the bear's happiness. Friendship was one solution. She agreed that as a result of our present dialogues she felt good about expressing her feelings and bringing them out in the open. It was good for people to open themselves up to others, unlike the way she had always been:

> *I think people should express [their feelings] because the more they keep it in, the more they're going to feel [lonely].*

Rosario also identified with the squirrel in the filmstrip who was hurt and needed shelter and care. The bear took care of the squirrel "day and night" until the squirrel had recovered. The bear's friendly relationship with the squirrel appeared to be the fulfillment of a deep need for relationships that were close, nurturing, and happy. Like the hurt squirrel, Rosario had needed care both night and day; warmth and caring at home; warm, caring friends outside the house; and support in school.

When the bear saw that the squirrel had recovered, the bear was happy; but sadness returned when he realized the squirrel might leave him. Rosario also longed for attachments but feared losing friendships and finding herself lonely again. Several circumstances prevented her from establishing relationships and friendships: her parents' busy schedule, the crowded conditions at home, the siblings not getting along, and the constant moving from school to school. Not only had Rosario been transplanted from the Philippines to the United States; she also had to endure moving to several different schools and classrooms during her elementary school years.

Rosario finally found a close friend when she was in the sixth or seventh grade. Her friend was also a Filipino girl; she is still Rosario's best friend. It took Rosario "seven years" to make a friend. This was an unusually long silent period.

> *It was nice having a friend so you could talk to her. I talked to her and told her some of my problems. She'd tell me hers.*

The primary theme in Rosario's film and in her life was loneliness. In the film she had created a fantasy world of friendship, caring, nurturing, and fun. But in her life she remained alone, distant, and closed.[7] Also, because Rosario missed the early experience of having friends, in later years she placed great value on friendships. In fact, she did not show up for one meeting with me because she had to take a friend to the hospital.[8]

During my dialogues with her, she blamed herself for not finishing school and "being lazy." But my sense was that she really was not to blame. When I asked her to read an article in a newspaper, she read and comprehended it well. Her inability to finish schooling was, I felt, more related to the fact that she had not received a strong educational foundation in her early years as she was moved around from school to school. She was given work she felt she could not handle. She lacked support from family members, and she lacked friends to validate her. Rosario was a child who had needed guidance and did not receive it. Had the school realized early that she was not receiving emotional support at home or at school, the staff might have been able to supply her with the support she was seeking and help her find a way to continue on to college. Her feelings needed to be acknowledged.

Remaining in exile. Today Rosario still longs to have finished her senior year with all her classmates. She is not acculturated into mainstream America; in essence, says George Wilson, she is a "Filipino in exile."[9] Those who have backgrounds in psychology understand that while Rosario is physically in this country, psychologically, her spirit is totally in the Philippines.

Dung (Yoong) Speaks

What had become of the 10-year-old Vietnamese child whose symbolic little egg incubated in a nest? She had heard from the others

---

[7] I was interested to know the effects of a child's long-term loneliness, the inability to make friends early in her life and to bond with any teacher at school. Grossenbacher (1988) commented: "Without friendships they do not get the validation from the outside that they need to get in touch with ways of validating themselves. It is very important [for children] to have friends so that they can experience a wide range of emotions without it being a great big deal. That is the normal thing with children. They get mad and the next day they are best friends. When they are cut off from that, they have terrible difficulties with relationships all their lives. It is important for them to feel safe in expressing feelings and to have those feelings validated."

[8] In Wilson's (1987) words: "She is like the lonely bear: whilst helping the squirrel, she helps herself. This is what is encouraging about her life now. With some schooling she could be in the helping professions because she is very nurturing, as symbolized by the bear who succeeds in getting the squirrel well. The bear earns friends through helping."

[9] In Wilson's (1987) words: "She needed support. Her feelings had to be included because, alienated and alone, she will only get overwhelmed. Society and her family failed her."

that I was in search of my former students. I had gone to the high school in search of her, and the administrators had contacted her. She appeared glad to see me again and when we met, she immediately recalled our time together at the Center. When I informed her that I was interested in talking with my former students about their film-strip stories, she volunteered enthusiastically. Our meetings took place in a classroom, at a restaurant, and in her apartment at a university campus. During the two-year period of our dialogues, I watched her develop from a high school student to a young college woman.

Dung's dramatic story unfolded from the time she was a 5-year-old immigrant child during the fall of Saigon in 1975. She recalled:

> It was a big mix-up. My dad and mom talked about it. They said the war is getting closer and closer to Saigon, and that's where I lived because my dad was in the navy and he had his base near there. He was on duty [as] a lieutenant commander.
>
> The day before he left [for duty] . . . I learned a few years later . . . they talked about there [was] going to be bombing, and my mom was to pack up and leave with the neighbor to the harbor and my dad would try to find us there and take us to his ship.
>
> Then there were four of us—my three brothers and I. I [was] the second . . . the only girl . . . over here we had a little sister.
>
> There was bombing that night. My mom packed up, went with the neighbors to the harbor, and we couldn't find my dad so we just followed the neighbors and we went into this big, big tank. I think it was an oil tanker . . . we stayed there that night.
>
> My dad was looking for us; "Have you seen my wife and kids?" he'd ask everybody. He'd go from ship to ship and look for us.
>
> My mom was thinking . . . she had to make these decisions without my dad. She . . . was not going . . . anywhere without my dad, so we got off the ship and we went onto another one and we were waiting and waiting.
>
> The ship was sailing too. We were going to leave without my father. A few minutes before the ship was sailing, my dad came and got us. What a relief that was, right? He took us to a war cruiser and told his men to go home to their families—there was nothing left, there was no more communication. Then the base blew up; it was a complete disaster. We went to a lot of islands before we came to America.

Culture shock. Dung went on to describe the difficulties she encountered in the U.S. school, primarily because she found that things were very different. In the beginning the schedule of classes confused her, because in Vietnam school began at 10 A.M. and went until 5 P.M., with a two-hour nap period. In the United States she started class at 7:45 A.M. and continued until 3:45 P.M. each day. She was often late to class and was punished by not being given the small rewards that other students received.

> *I couldn't adjust. I'd go to school late. I remember every week on Friday after school, the teacher would give little presents to kids that were good during the week. And if you were tardy, you wouldn't get a present. If you misbehaved, you wouldn't get a present. And it would be like a little piece of candy or something like that, or a little toy. I would never get one because I would always come to school late, and that hurt at first. I had a terrible time. I didn't look forward to going to school.*

Perhaps if the teacher had known that Dung had just experienced the horrors of war, the teacher might have supported her more and her tardiness would have diminished. Neither parents nor teacher knew the struggle she was undergoing during this period of adjustment to the new country. The 5-year-old child transported from a war-torn country had to try to fit in on her own.

Dung spoke of Vietnamese schools as being serious and strict:

> *In kindergarten in Vietnam you would learn how to read and write. And no playing . . . you have to recite stories and things like that.*
>
> *I remember getting hit for sitting in the wrong way. I was sitting . . . one of my legs up on the bench and the teacher came by, whack! I knew why I got hit. They don't tell you why. You're supposed to know yourself.*
>
> *And then I came over here. I was too quick in kindergarten . . . all I did there was play . . . in Vietnam you do not play.*
>
> *I was sitting there and I was like, "this is not for me" and I wouldn't play with them. And so the teachers put me up to first grade . . . it was better there than in kindergarten. In kindergarten I felt they were treating me like a little girl.*
>
> *In the first grade . . . I couldn't adjust still then because the kids would treat me differently because I wouldn't know how to speak English and at that school there weren't many Vietnamese students. I was just all by myself.*
>
> *The teachers were nice, but it was hard because I couldn't communicate with them—it was hard to adjust. I'd go to school late. The teacher would get upset about it. I think I tried telling her why . . . that didn't help much. She just said this is the rule. You have to do this. I'd always wake up late and I'd always go to school late.*

Dung's adjustment was also complicated by moving constantly from class to class and school to school. She tried to fit into kindergarten, then first grade, and then went to various summer schools to speed up her acquisition of English. As a result she felt insecure.

> *Moving a lot didn't help me very much to grow up to be secure and settled. I needed to be set in one place and to grow. It was too much moving around.*

Need for friends. Dung skipped second grade entirely and went to third and fourth grade at a multiracial school with "a lot of cultures" and friendly students of several nationalities. In this school she found friends who made things easier for her:

> *I was surprised that I enjoyed school . . . and I made lots of friends. I even had a really close friend, a best friend, that lived near my house, and we did everything together.*

Dung didn't mention whether her neighborhood friend was Vietnamese. She just said that the girl was her "best friend . . . and we did everything together." Life then began to have a brighter side. The warmth of friendship sustained her, even though her friend wasn't in the same school. I had come to know Dung in the fifth grade at the Center, where she wrote about her friendship with this neighbor. In her stories she wrote about her adventures with her friend as they sat together in a "flying rainbow." Together they visited many places.

On days when Dung had felt safe to be her Vietnamese self at the Center, she had asked if she could listen to Vietnamese music on her Walkman cassette player while reviewing her English spelling lesson. I debated with myself but thought I would grant her permission. How her face lit up as she wiggled and moved to the music while observing and going over the varying structure of the English language. She was far away then from the days when she would get a "whack" for sitting in the wrong position or would be deprived of a reward for being late. She was happy in her own world. She was a delight to watch.

Dung's mother had insisted that she study the Vietnamese language during summers. She had to stay home and study while other children played. As a child she resented having to study Vietnamese, but later she valued her ability to read and write Vietnamese.

I had observed her innovative and artistic abilities. She commented later:

> *I loved creating things by myself. I still do. I take photography and it's going to be a hobby for me. . . . I love arranging flowers because all of these things let me create things from pictures in*

*my mind. I love creating. And I like it when it's from me and
from no one else. I can't stand it when someone tells me, "No,
no, you're not supposed to do it this way or that way, this way."
I want it to be from me, not anybody else. That's why I wanted
to make [my filmstrips all] by myself.*

I had already reflected about *The Little Egg* filmstory while observing Dung at the Center. Now she was going to take me through the
symbols herself.

The silent stage/incubation. Dung recalled that she had put all her
"feelings into that little filmstrip . . . there was so much message in
that story." The two years of incubation represented the two years
when she was silent and unable to communicate with anyone at
school. The egg was alone in the nest.

*The little egg, that was me at M. P. Brown [school]. It was terri-
ble. I was a little egg and the whole world was around me. . . . I
was in the shelter, and it cracked. I didn't know what to do.*

Dung, as a child, figuratively suggested how to resolve the problem by expressing the need for an environment in which she could
feel safe and grow. She suggested a teacher who would understand
her. Tai-Hing was a "wish" teacher of the same culture. Dung, now
older, explained:

*Vietnam was my heritage and I wanted to keep it. Someday I
hope to return for a visit. The first year in America, the time just
lagged. No one could understand me. I had a terrible time. I
couldn't communicate with anyone. I couldn't even tell my parents my problem because they were adapting too. I was that little
egg, and the whole world was around me. I was in a shelter. I
felt I needed that shelter, for I was lost and afraid. I was also
insecure. I developed an insecurity complex because I couldn't
do things by myself.
    The egg cracked open one day and turned into a beautiful
bird. That was my hope, my wish. That everything would turn
out okay someday. I was afraid I was not going to make it then.
    The bird flew to Tai-Hing, who represented the person I
wished I had to help me grow up and adapt to American society.
With the problem of insecurity, I needed someone to care for me, to
hold my hand and say, "It's all right, I'll help you. Don't be
afraid." I needed someone to set me on the right track. I needed her
caring so that I could be stronger. I just needed her caring so that I
could begin to do things on my own. So that is why Tai-Hing let
the bird go when the bird got bigger. I believed that all stories
should have a happy ending, getting married and staying happy.*

Living in two worlds. Dung felt the stress of living in two cultures, two worlds. She explained:

> There is more freedom here than in Vietnam. Over here I do one thing and my friends at school do another. It's hard. I want what they have. It's hard to just mix them together. I couldn't do what other kids were doing, and that was hard. I couldn't understand them [then]. But I do now.

If only the understanding had been mutual so that Dung's friends could have understood her background, could have learned to pronounce her name as Dung had to learn, with great difficulty, to pronounce theirs. She spoke here of being on the outside of a culture that did not understand her. To adapt then, she changed her name to "Christine" so that she would be accepted, and because Americans mispronounced her Vietnamese name and that embarrassed her. She was doing all the changing, all the adapting, and in so doing she experienced a loss of identity.

Need for recognition. At home she felt that the Vietnamese culture focused greater attention on the boys. Her need to be recognized spurred her to work hard in school. In school, however, she felt she was far behind her classmates and despaired that she would never catch up:

> I was trying to catch up. [When] it [was] time to move on, I wasn't up there. I was down [here] still trying to pick it up.
>   I had a really, really insecure personality because of the change in my life. And I couldn't adjust to any of it. When it was time to move on to the next stage, I was still behind.

Even though Dung began earning A grades from seventh grade on, in high school she felt insecure. She was clever enough to take classes that were below her ability so she could maintain her straight A average:

> I played a trick on everybody. When I enrolled in the class, they gave me a test. I'd do badly so I could stay in the class.

In Dung's sophomore year she finally began to feel some confidence and began taking college prep classes. This resulted in another problem, because in the process she was no longer with her supportive friends. In her junior year she finally felt she was able to do well and had gotten a handle on her insecurity. By her senior year she was a member of the California Scholarship Federation and graduated with honors.

She attributes her success to the care she felt from others: "people who sat down and talked to me when I was confused."

> I had my counselors. I had my teachers. I had a lot of people who cared. I had my friends who cared. They gave [me] encouragement . . . a lot of encouragement. My parents were a great help too. They expected a lot of me so I would be successful.

Caught between two cultures. In our dialogues Dung explained that once she felt secure with her friends and teachers in high school, she began to open up and share her feelings with them. She no longer had to be like the egg hiding in a shelter. She felt a lot freer when she was able to share her experiences in Vietnam and her early experiences in America.

Dung's cultural conflict had been more severe when she first arrived:

> I didn't know which way to act—the way I was raised or the way everybody else was acting. It was like I was a mixture of the two, and I didn't know what to do. One minute I'm this, and another minute I'm that. I couldn't put it all together. . . . That's why I was so insecure.

At the time of our dialogues, Dung became aware of her cultural conflict and began the process of integration. She felt she was a Vietnamese American. Vietnamese first, American second. Her wish was to return to Vietnam for a visit—the Vietnam from which she had to flee for her life:

> I want to go back there—I mean, not to stay—I love America and this is my home—but I want to go back there, and I want to share my experience with everybody back there who hasn't had the chance to come over here. I know it's really hard over there because I still have relatives.

As Dung and I concluded our dialogues, she came to a career decision. She wanted to be a children's dentist. She expressed with exuberance, "I love kids; I love, love, love kids, yeah."

The Children's Messages to the Teachers

QIU LIANG

> They should be more patient [with an immigrant child] because it is very difficult for a person to be in a new country and learn a new language. Have patience.

*If the teacher feels there is no hope in an immigrant child,
then the child will think, "Well, if the teacher who's helping me
thinks that I can't go anywhere, then I might as well give up
myself." Because in his heart he thinks that the teacher will not
help me, and there's no one else around that he can turn to.
Because all he thinks is that the teacher is the closest friend, in a
way, that he knows, and now the teacher even gets tired of helping him or her, then this person will give up.*

*The most important thing is for the teacher to have patience
and for the student to think positively. If you think negative,
eventually it will turn out that you cannot do it.*

*I myself always thought that I could do it and that I would
get through one day. And now I finally got through.*

Teachers Need to Understand Other Cultures' Attitudes toward Teachers

In my experience, many immigrant children throughout the
world, not just Asians, bring with them the attitude that they must
render respect and obedience to the teacher in the same way they
respect their parents. When children leave home, they are entrusted
to the teacher. Teachers then become their "educational parents." The
teacher becomes not only an ally but a person whose voice is respected and obeyed. Qiu Liang described how immigrant children
bring this deeply ingrained attitude to school in America and how
they quickly pick up and obey the conscious or unconscious attitudes
of their teachers. They may even misread the teachers because of
cultural differences or because the teachers are often rushed. Irrita-
tion or exhaustion from an overloaded work day may be misread as a
sign of not caring.

ALICE

*I think schools should encourage students to try to help the im-
migrant children as much as they can.*

*'Til today, I still hear some of my friends saying how they
felt when they just came here . . . left out . . . and so I think every
immigrant [should be made to feel part of the group].*

*I don't think there will ever be a way [for schools to ease the
pain so kids can learn]. I mean, until today there's still discrimination against people from other countries. I think it will be better, but it will never be out of the way.*

*[To put new immigrant arrivals together] would have helped.
I would have felt probably more secure. I would have had someone to talk to, for one thing.*

Teachers Need to Understand How the
U.S. Educational System Discriminates against "The Other"

Alice, in her wisdom, was implying that schools have been unprepared to meet the needs of the large number of immigrant children. The psychological trauma that she hinted at was less visible, less easily measured, than her language proficiency. She is an example of how schools have not yet learned how to integrate immigrant children into the U.S. educational system. I agree with Raoufi that we must not treat immigrant children as " 'accidental and temporary guests' " (1981, page 132). "Left out," as Alice described it—for it takes longer to establish a feeling of well-being than it does to learn a second language.

CINDY

Try to understand the background of the individual students, because each country teaches the students to act in certain ways. Explain that even though a student is getting a C, it doesn't mean that he can't do it; it's going to take time to learn the process because sometimes it gets kids down to know that they can't do as well as the other kids.

I think that if I were an elementary school teacher and I had kids coming in from other countries, I would try really hard to understand their background first and somehow need to realize that it's different, of course, a lot different here than in their old country and it's a whole different environment.

I think at that age it's really important for them [kids] to know that everybody makes mistakes, because when you first arrive, you get discouraged from your mistakes.

Children don't express what they feel verbally and so would be upset or real quiet. If teachers can tell something is bothering them . . . they [should] try to get it out of them.

I went through a stage where I was thinking I don't understand what they are saying to me, when am I going to be able to communicate back to them? [It] kinda made me confused and unsure exactly whether I'm going to be able to reach that point. So I think it's little talks that help [them] realize that if [they] put enough into it, that you reach that something. I did have a counselor [at the school]. Everything that first year went from my teacher to Linda, then to me. I think the teacher would basically have to tell me, not the counselor, that I was going to make it.

Teachers Need to Understand the
Cultural Background of Immigrant Students

Thinking they are not going to "make it" is a recurring theme with all the children who spoke. They keep this feeling inside. Teachers in their eagerness to help may try to communicate through a translator. But children raised in a culture of "whatever teacher says is right" wait for the moment in which the teacher himself or herself will ease their frustration about making it. Not receiving communication from the teacher promotes anxiety in the child. Cindy makes it very clear that not her peers, not the counselor, but the teacher is the person who eases things for her. The teacher, in turn, needs to set up the curriculum so that the child can succeed in school.

When I ask a teacher to try to understand the background of the student, I am also suggesting that the adult intervene so that the child can make a transition. "If teacher understands, then I'll feel better," says the child. And if understood, the child doesn't feel discounted.

Teachers Need to Understand the Teaching Methods and Educational System in the Student's Home Country

Another issue is the matter of teaching method. The child, confused by different teaching styles in the host country as compared to his or her own country, asks, "Did my teacher in Hong Kong teach me the wrong way? Is the method here better than in Hong Kong? Do I discount the manner in which I learned in my country? Is the new teacher interested in me?"

Cindy gave the teacher permission to intervene in her quiet behavior and to try to find out what was bothering her. It's almost as if she were saying, "The way I was taught [was that] I shouldn't speak. The way you were taught [you] can. So reach out to me and show me how to come out."

ROSARIO

Stop and help them for a while. Try to understand how they feel. Helping me through even though I made so many mistakes—still help me.

I would tell them [teachers] to understand how it feels to be an immigrant child. I would try to listen to them and [not] rush them. Help them to be successful by giving them things they can do and not things they cannot do . . . and help them find friends. Be patient and encourage them.

It's better to open up and tell them [the teachers] your problems.

Immigrant Students Need to Feel Valued and Accepted

From an educator's point of view, Rosario had not been successful academically. From the point of view of the psychologists, she had not undergone the process of acculturation or adaptation into a new society. Nevertheless, her story moved me to spend many long hours with her beyond the time scheduled for dialogues. Without the tape recorder keeping track of her every word, she was a warm and articulate person who could read and comprehend what she was reading. She also had the ability to provide deep insights into the characters of a story I asked her to read. She undoubtedly has the capacity of going beyond where she left off academically.

The message to give immigrant children, the message they must feel, is that they are important and lovable just as they are, and that learning a new language is merely adding to what they know, helping them become communicative in more than one way. More than anything else, the immigrant child needs friendship, companions, warmth, and continued renewal and connection to his or her roots.

DUNG

Try to get them to talk to you. Not just everyday conversation, but what they feel inside. Try to get them to get that out, because it's hard for kids. They don't trust—I had a hard time trusting and I was really insecure because of that.

Just talk, just talk with the student. Get a closer relationship with your student. Because the teacher is an important person in the child's life. The teacher is the person who the student is going to look up to in school. And the kid is in school most of the time.

You learn a lot from school and in school, not just study, work, and things like that, but about life. The person who's going to guide the student helps the student develop a good personality, good insight of who she is, who the kid is. The kid looks up [to the teacher].

The teacher is that person who is there to help the child. But that person is not that much help if he can't communicate with [the immigrant student]. Putting an immigrant child who doesn't speak English into a classroom, a regular classroom with American students, is not very good. It scares the hell out of her or him because it is so different. [Teachers] should start [them] slowly and have special classes where the child could adapt and learn a little bit about American society and customs.

Teachers Need to Be Models and "Educational Parents" Whom Immigrant Children Can Trust

Dung explained in her own way the concept of teacher as "educational parent"—the one who not only teaches but helps the student to develop a good personality. The teacher should be a person whom the student admires and emulates and with whom he or she can share deep feelings—a trusted adult.

Thoughts about
Themes from the Dialogues

Qiu Liang (Dennis): Integrating Two Cultures

Although all five of the children had profited from working in the Center, only Qiu Liang (Dennis) had been able to develop an integrated sense of self. Because he was allowed sufficient "sheltered" time in the Center, the threefold cultural/academic/psychological (CAP) intervention could take place. This is what the next part of the book addresses. As Qiu Liang faced the challenges of silence, isolation, resistance to change, vulnerability, helplessness, exhaustion, feelings of hopelessness, feelings of difference, fear of ridicule, inner repression of his native culture, and problems in adjusting to the new culture, the place, time, and warmth of the surroundings—along with the direct cultural, academic, and psychological interventions— facilitated his adjustment. Through the filmstrips, Dennis and I found a way to harness his creativity so that he could express some of the feelings that beset him. Through this medium he could communicate with me and with the world around him. Dennis gradually came to integrate his two selves—Chinese and new American—as well as to learn subject matter and improve his linguistic skills. By the time he had reached college age, he was a secure individual who knew who he was: a Chinese man who lived and studied in the United States and was able to speak both English and Chinese with fluency. Dennis was indeed fully alive.

Alice: Cultural Split/
Pressure to Assimilate

Even though Alice is Qiu Liang's sister, she has been unable to integrate her cultural split. Her time in the Center had been limited. Before coming to the Center, Alice had felt strongly the need to assimilate to avoid the name-calling and teasing from children who did not realize their own cruelty and who were not aware of the advantages of getting to know children from different cultures.

Alice struggled with culture shock and retreated inside herself. She was silent and felt lonely, defensive, angry, and helpless. In the

Center she was a good student and learned English easily, but she did not feel competent. At that time she felt a complete split between her life at home, where she spoke Chinese, and her life in school, where she hid her "Chineseness" and tried to be as American as possible.

At the time of our dialogues, I met her in front of the school. I was surprised to see an outgoing, extroverted person when I recalled her as timid, hesitant, and serious at the Center—her cultural split was quite visible. When we had a chance to speak about the matter, she expressed the desire to become more of a bilingual person and be able to integrate both worlds.

Cindy: Cultural Split/Loss of Native Language and Culture

Cindy, too, retained a cultural split, although as she entered college she showed some evidence of being able to process and integrate both cultures. Her original culture shock was not as great as that of Dennis or Alice because (1) she had been exposed to Western culture in Hong Kong, and (2) when she came to the United States she moved into the home of her grandparents, who were American citizens.

Cindy was acutely aware of her inability to socialize with the children in the "mainstream" classes. Although her initial reaction to the new country had been one of excitement and curiosity, she soon became depressed as she felt the pressure to adapt and experienced the loss of her native language and culture. She had difficulty adjusting to a different, less rigid type of school system. In the Center, Cindy like Alice, had learned to confront some of the shyness and silence that were the result of her previous cultural conditioning.

Cindy was comfortable with the English language. Her task as an adult was to regain her Chinese self. As she became older and more mature, she discovered that she did not want to keep that vital part of her nature buried. Cindy was "in process" toward becoming an integrated person.

Rosario: Unintegrated/"In Exile"— Unrooted in Either Culture

Rosario had been in the Center for only one period per day. She had always worked in a group with other children. Her great need to fill the gaps in her education and to connect with her peers was not expressed except in the filmstrip *The Lonely Bear*. She had no one teacher or counselor to work with her sufficiently to help bridge the gap between her two cultures. She could not find support at home, where the stress of the immigration process sapped the energy of both parents. The father, who was tired and not communicative when he came home, went to bed early to gain the strength to work the next day. Her family did not recognize her depression and blamed her for what they considered "her failure" in school. Rosario felt that if her sympathetic counselor had remained in her high school until her senior year, she would have graduated. As it turned out, Rosario was left with a feeling of personal inadequacy. She remains "in exile" from her native land without putting down strong roots in her present environment. Her transplant has not yet taken hold.

Dung: Cultural Split: Outwardly Successful/ Inwardly Insecure—The Need for Support

Although bright and successful academically, Dung still is not able to integrate her Vietnamese and American selves. She, too, has a cultural split. Both Dung and Cindy are examples of students whose psychological and cultural trauma is hidden because they have been able to be successful academically. The children needed extended time in one classroom, with one teacher who would have known to intervene where necessary. It was difficult for an outsider to see that Dung felt "insecure," that she felt she was a "mixture of two and didn't know what to do."

Dung's story emphasizes the need for immigrant children to have sufficient experience with an "educational parent" who will shelter them until their roots sink deep into the new soil and become strong—strong enough so they can retain their original cultures while adapting to the new one.

Differences among Immigrant Childrens' Experiences

The Unintegrated Inner World

Rosario's experience in school was a painful one: seven years without a friend and only "squirrels" to comfort the "lonely bear." Her story should jar us into seeing one of the strongest reasons to radically change the school system. Deep down, Rosario wanted to succeed—all children want to succeed. The hope in her story was that she did have the initiative to find friends outside her home and outside school. Also, her work sustained her, but she could have used more support.

The Culturally Split Inner World

Cultural split begins when the child has to behave one way at home and another way at school. It is the setting aside of one's past so that one can adapt an American persona. A cultural split is a wound, because part of oneself is lost to the other part. It is my observation and experience that the cultural split begins very early in children's school life—as early as kindergarten, when their cultures are not validated in school and they feel isolated from the others.

Alice, Cindy, and Dung closed off their cultural selves and re-awoke to them during our later dialogues. They then began the process of regaining what had been lost. The regaining is like a wound wanting to heal. The experiences of their native culture and language were like the wood in a fireplace where the fire has been temporarily snuffed out, but the embers are still burning—banked, but alive.

The Integrated Inner World

Qiu Liang's (Dennis's) experience is like the wood in a fireplace where the fire has been kept alive to become a stronger flame. The fire blazes up because the student is ready and the opportunity presents itself.

Reconnecting

The Five Children, Now Adults

As I give closure to the pages of this first part of the book, you may want to know how the five children who provided insights and messages for teachers have progressed as young adults.

Qiu Liang is 26 years old. He has completed his degree in advertising and works in a company. He has his own apartment and is making plans to purchase his own home. He is energetic, interested in people, well liked, and quite busy in life. He leaves us with no more messages. He has said it all.

Alice is 24 years old. She graduated from the university with a B.A. in art. She majored in graphic design and minored in photography. There is an energetic joy about her as she begins to look for work. She speaks:

*There is always a sense of wanting to hide a part of myself that
other people feel is different or foreign. But lately, I feel I can be
more open about my language and culture. I am more confident.*

*My parents wanted to send me to a Chinese school, but as a
kid I did not want it. Looking back, I regret not having studied it
(written Chinese). It would make me feel a lot better if I had the
ability to write it. But I am happy that I do speak it fluently.*

Cindy is 24 years old. She graduated from the university with a
B.A. in social welfare and a minor in psychology. She has a full-time
job as a social worker where she is in contact with immigrant Chinese. She is "regaining" her language as she speaks Chinese every day.
She also works at the family store on Saturdays. She speaks:

*It is important to maintain one's culture and language. It is all
a part of one's identity. Without it I am in the middle, sitting on
a fence, neither a part of the Chinese community, who see me as
ABC (American-born Chinese), nor the American community,
who see me as Chinese. It is important for parents to help their
children maintain their cultural identity. But each day, I am regaining what was lost.*

Rosario is 24 years old. She has a friend and a child and she is surrounded by the warmth of her family, now settled immigrants. She
feels that she is now a Filipino American after receiving her citizen-
ship papers. She has a part-time job working in a store and a part-
time job doing social work. Her life is full. She is silent about school.

Dung is 24 years old. She is now married. She took a year and a
half off from the university but has now returned to complete her
degree in pediatric nursing. Her life is filled with work and study. She
speaks:

*My family wanted to keep the old tradition separate from the rest
of the United States. One can retain one's culture and cultural
identity, but eventually one must integrate both cultures. At first
I needed to act one way at home and another way at school. I
got older, I moved away from my family for a while. Then I
began to communicate with my parents and together we began
to come to a resolution.*

*I have integrated both cultures. I do not feel I have a cul-
tural split because I feel at the core I am Vietnamese American. I
think the key is communication.*

*I married a Chinese man and I live in a multicultural area.
I feel at home with myself. I look at people as individuals.*

Summary

Friendships are very important for children. Guide them and provide the time for them to form friendships. Talk about the characteristics that make for genuine friendship.

Take time to talk about why discrimination happens and how to prevent it from happening.

Encourage children to bring feelings out into the open. Point out the difference between everyday conversations and expressing what they feel inside.

Teach the children to be inclusive of others.

Preserve the cultural identity of the children; bring out their mother tongue; let them be comfortable speaking their own language without excluding others. Let them enjoy the sounds of the languages of other children.

Try speaking some of their languages. Let the children enjoy how you struggle with their language. They will feel "smarter than the teacher."

Parents need support in helping their children preserve their culture. Dung's parents wanted her to study Vietnamese, but the child resisted. If the school values the child's original language, the child will value it at home, too.

Let them bring their native clothing to school. Let them wear it in the classroom. Allow some time for them to sit at their desks and work so that they do not feel shame, so that they feel it is natural to wear their native clothing. These are not costumes but living symbols of their origins.

Learn to speak a second language so that you understand from experience how a second language adds to your own.

Take care to speak to the children in a manner that does not negate their need to master the English language. Children can be very literal, and by encouraging children to preserve and speak their native language, they can become fearful of learning English because they may fear losing their mother tongue.

When the children have become very articulate in English, they may feel that they have forgotten their native language. But the mother tongue can be easily accessible with practice. Assure them that they have the potential to learn both.

At first, time will lag—get them involved as much as possible and check for ways to close the academic gaps if there are any.

Find ways to show the children that they can make it. "Give them things that they can do, not things that they cannot do" (Rosario), but at the same time, give them challenging work.

Entering Part II of This Book

I take with me to my next experience all that I have learned from the children. I try to apply what I know and begin the process of rethinking my teaching.

Having understood Qui Liang's (Dennis's) acculturation process, would it be possible for me to apply what I had learned to an entire class? In the following pages, join me again to meet children from other cultural backgrounds. I invite you to listen to what the children have to say and to enter into a teacher's struggles and joys in the work with immigrant children.

Teaching Immigrant Students: Integrating the Cultural/Academic/ Psychological Dimensions of the Whole Child

4

Cultural/ Academic/ Psychological Interventions

Good morning, teacher. Thanks for your helping us. You are a very kind teacher and peaceful. I did my spelling, math and history, but I got little problems about it. If you please help me that the words that I don't know. Please call me and solve my problems.

BOY FROM AFGHANISTAN, AGE 11

In these simple but moving words an Afghan boy expressed both what he needs and what he thinks he needs. He believes that the teacher can solve his problems, and this is partially true. He needs the academic intervention that would make him feel a deeper sense of power. On the other hand, he has to learn how to solve his own academic "problems" in order to gain the confidence that will be

113

his strength during the rest of his academic years. The fact that he knows how to ask for help is a good beginning.

When I work with immigrant children, I think carefully about all the cultures in the room. I begin by being aware of the potential learning situation. A sensitive understanding of one's students is the key to whether the blocked energies of a youngster will unblock. I am always interested in the end result and ready to give up on an old idea or approach, if I see it isn't working. No two lesson plans are the same each year. There is no formula that works all the time; everything really depends on the children. I listen to them. I observe them in the schoolyard, while I am teaching a lesson, or when we are working in small groups. I am always looking out of the corner of my eye. I can even see around corners.

Attempting to Apply Theory to Practice

Some years after my work with the children from the Center, and after I had completed my doctorate, I took a position teaching "mainstream" children in a suburban school; but I always heard, as if from a distance, the voices of immigrant children calling to me. This call became too strong for me not to answer. I moved to a teaching position in a school where the students were from many countries, including Afghanistan, Fiji, Mexico, Egypt, the Philippines, the Ukraine, El Salvador, and Poland. The children had been placed in a "Sheltered English" class in which I was the teacher.

I started the job enthusiastically. The children had been in this country for a minimum of one year to a maximum of six. Many of them had been in sheltered or mainstream classes year after year but were still unable to keep up to grade level. They needed a "nest."

The "messages" from my former students allowed me to rethink my teaching. The smile of F'aatui and the look in his eyes as we discovered that storytelling was still a useful and respected tool; the boy from Guam who stayed overtime to "become a student"—these images and voices became embedded in my mind. I was eager to be with the children as they "shot the wolves and tigers" and stared back at those "yellow eyes"; to encourage lonely little girls to find friendships more readily so they would not have to put "Xs" on drawings to keep "little bananas" company. I would teach the "squirrels" to nurture each other and warm their own nests so the "incubating eggs" could hatch into "beautiful birds." I had been in dialogue with immigrant children, anthropologists, linguists, sociologists, psychologists, and teachers. Now I was ready for the adventure.

Then came the cold light of reality! I visited my new school and saw the bare cupboards of my classroom. The only books available were fifth and sixth grade textbooks (which none of the children could read). A few old basal readers could be checked out from the school library, but not enough so each student could have a copy. A few storybooks could also be checked out, but these would have to be returned. The school district was in deep financial trouble. I had known about the poverty of this school district, but I had not expected to enter an empty classroom devoid of books and learning materials. It was a tremendous letdown.

The principal was sympathetic and offered to ask teachers to redistribute their materials—which, unfortunately, would leave some teachers without sufficient books and supplies for their own established programs. The teachers who were hoarding feared the "famine" they had already experienced when they first came to the school. Not wanting to alienate them, I decided against taking anything from them. Teachers who had been in the school longer had an unwritten policy: "I begged and borrowed, and so must you."

Had this been my first teaching assignment, I would have placed the keys to my room on the principal's desk and turned in my resignation. I thought about doing just that for three days. I despaired as the opening of school quickly approached. In my journal I wrote:

> I work in a school where police records show that 80 percent of the city's crimes are committed within 10 blocks of the school. I have a total of 27 immigrant children. I have one ream of paper a month, no spelling books, no readable language arts books, no science books, no scissors, no rulers. I have the knowledge and experience to help these children in transition, but no tools. We are in trouble.

What impelled me to stay? Perhaps I wanted to stand by and watch how the students would confront those "yellow eyes." I liked the challenge. Perhaps I heeded the artist within me and allowed my imaginative nature to find a way to paint even with the most rudimentary brushes and colors. Calling forth my creative energy, I drummed up every bit of teaching experience and imagination I had to enter into this adventure with the children—a chance to expand and develop the art of pedagogy.

It is easy to teach when one simply follows prescribed teaching methods and does not enter the inner world of the children. But I had behind me the experience at the Center and was enlightened by the insights gained there. I was grateful to those children and felt a strong sense of responsibility toward them and toward my new students. In this school I needed to shape my teaching to come to a balance between the ideal and the real.

"Sheltered English" was the district's classification of my class. Sheltered English, they said, was an instructional approach used to make academic instruction in English understandable to "limited-English proficient students"—a term that does not describe the whole child. Students in these classes were "sheltered" in that they did not compete academically with native English speakers. In the regular classroom, English fluency is assumed. In Sheltered English, class teachers use physical activities, visual aids, and the environment to teach important new words for concept development in math, science, history, and other subjects. English instruction is the key element in Sheltered English.

As I was enlightened by the children at the Center, my Sheltered English students, immigrants who shared no common language, were to learn to read and write in English, filling in whatever language and academic gaps they had developed. In the context of learning English, they were to maintain their own cultures in order to prevent cultural splits and to learn about each other's cultures as well. As their skills improved and as they were ready, they would learn the history and mores of the host country as well as the rest of the required curriculum for their grade and age. Always my focus for them was to be on their ability to become literate—both in English and in their native language whenever possible.

In my mind "Sheltered English" was an apt name because the class would become a place where the children could, as Dung had said, "stay in one place and grow."

According to the plan suggested by the district, the immigrant children would be mainstreamed into regular classes for art, music, and physical education, the subjects least linguistically demanding. This plan did not work. The children from mainstream and sheltered classes worked together in art, music, and physical education to speed up the non-native speakers' integration of cultures and acquisition of English; but because these classes were taught only once or twice a week by teachers who did not know the immigrant children, both groups of children, "mainstream" and sheltered, fought and stole from each other, and cultural conflicts resulted. I preferred the plan to keep them in a self-contained classroom and to allow me to get to know each child personally. I prepared them to develop and integrate their individual worlds first before mixing them all together. Inner integration for me is far more effective than outer. In the former, the child is "at home" with himself or herself and therefore is free to allow others to be themselves. In the latter, integration occurs only by chance. I pause briefly from my story to explain an approach I used with the children in the sheltered classroom that evolved from my practice and insights from the children at the Center. It has to do with intervention.

From Practice Comes Theory: Evolving a Cultural/Academic/Psychological (CAP) Approach to Teaching Immigrant Children

To intervene is to mediate. It is to act as an intermediary between extremes, to interact with a person to facilitate his or her own reconciliation of opposites within himself (or herself). Combining the idea of intervention with the children's need to communicate—to "talk, talk, not just about everyday things, but feelings," as Dung had said— I used a method I called *dialogic intervention*, which addresses the feelings of the child through the development of a close relationship and continuous dialogue between the child and teacher. With this process, I could intervene or act as a mediator in and respond to individual students' cultural, academic, and psychological needs and concerns.

Beginning with Dialogic Intervention

Dialogic intervention is a way by which caring parents, family members, friends, and counselors can mediate so that the person can open up the blocked energies within. It is a way to assist the person to see that there are two sides of a coin: that there are opposites, and where one sees only the negative aspect of a situation, the positive is always present and waiting to be tapped. If a teacher listens closely to what the children are saying, she or he can often hear the negatives that block their progress.

Young children have a tendency to be concrete and literal. They can get stuck in one way of thinking without realizing it until someone intervenes. Also, what goes on inside the mind of a child is not always known by the adult or the teacher. If children feel the affection of the teacher, it becomes easier for them to open up. The teacher can act as an intermediary between the child's thinking and reality.

Some examples of dialogic intervention in the classroom follow:

Child: I can't spell.
Teacher: You can spell your name.

Child: I can't read.
Teacher: You just read that word.

Child: I can't write.
Teacher: And you just wrote that sentence.

Child: Everyone's going to laugh at me.

Teacher: That boy just passed by and he didn't laugh.

Child: I am afraid to learn English because I might forget my language.

Teacher: And you are capable of learning two.

Soon the children themselves intervene with each other:

Child: My drawing is no good.

Child: I like it, it is pretty.

When an entire class begins to be aware of the positive aspects of situations, then there is a lot of good energy in the room because transformations begin to take place. It is not enough to say, "don't think that way"; instead, it is best to show the other side so the child can see, feel, and rethink.

The rationale for dialogic intervention came directly from the children:

> *That's how I came here. I was shy to say what I wanted to say. Even though I wanted to speak, I would never raise my hand or say what I thought. Because [in my country] they don't encourage you to speak out what you feel or think. In my mind I took it that we should keep things to ourselves.* [Need for cultural intervention]

> *I think the teacher would basically have to tell me that I would make it in school . . . that I'll finally get it.* [Need for academic intervention]

> *When you first arrive, you get discouraged from your mistakes because kids compare and you feel bad inside. Many children do not express what they feel verbally and so they would be upset or be real quiet and you can tell that something is bothering them. Try to get it out of them.* [Need for psychological intervention]

My use of dialogic intervention led to the evolution of an intervention approach that is interdisciplinary and threefold: cultural/academic/psychological (CAP). I use the acronym to name the approach but in no way to suggest it to be a formula. The threefold intervention (CAP) is not meant to focus on dialogue alone, but on whatever form—art, music, journals, and so forth—the children need to give them an integrated sense of self and a feeling of well-being in the classroom.

In her journal, a child wrote:

Today when I came to school I was very happy. Then when my teacher was working with us, I would get the answers wrong. I was sad. I was thinking that I was stupid. But then my teacher was talking to me. I was feeling better. I am very happy in my classroom. I want to stay here in my classroom with my teacher and friends.

GIRL FROM AFGHANISTAN, AGE 11

Rationale for the CAP Intervention

I see the cultural and psychological aspects as the foundation of the intervention. They point to and clear the way for academic intervention and academic achievement. The circle represents the whole child. When the child feels in balance with these three aspects of herself or himself, the child in school is fully alive.

Teaching the whole child presents a challenge, because focusing on the cultural and psychological aspects of these children may cause the academic to begin to fade into the background. Such was the case with a girl from Afghanistan who spent most of her school years wrestling within herself, with her Muslim American cultural split, and feeling unhappy because she was not able to succeed academically in school. But as she began to accept her Muslim traditions she quieted down, and through a rigorous academic program (which I

The Threefold Intervention

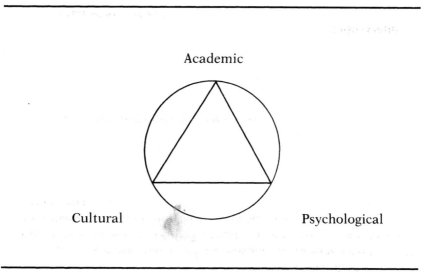

Academic

Cultural   Psychological

will describe later) she began to feel successful in school. She wrote in her school journal:

> *Do you know that I am learning so much in this classroom? I*
> *have been in America for six years and this is my first year that*
> *I have been learning so much.*

Of course, it is possible for even culturally happy children to be unable to read or write and unable to integrate academically in the mainstream. On the other hand, we have also seen (in the case of Alice) that if the focus is merely on academics, a cultural-psychological split and maladjustment result—"at home I act one way and at school, another way." The difficulty about the triangle is that two sides may exert pressure to leave the third aspect out. It takes skill and consciousness on the part of the teacher to keep the balance. When I meet an immigrant child for the first time and when we are in dialogue, in my mind I ask myself questions whose answers might reveal the need for cultural, academic, and psychological interventions. Some of these are:

> How does the child feel about his or her country?
> How does he or she feel about leaving the homeland?
> What can be done to maintain his or her language?
> How does the child feel about school?
> Does the child have friends?
> What is the child's academic background?

Sometimes I focus on the cultural, then the psychological, then both, but I always keep the academic clearly in focus so the child understands its importance in school.

CAP Intervention in Practice

On that first day of class, the children lined up outside. They always behave perfectly on the first day, as they are eager to know something about their teacher and how things will "work." It is on this day that I set the expectations for the year.

Students entered the classroom and engaged in nervous chatter; many spoke to each other in their native languages. I observed an Afghan boy wearing a baseball cap backwards, his hands on his hips, trying to talk like an American kid. "What's goin' on, man?" he asked. I could tell by his accent that he was a recent arrival.

Here was a chance for my first cultural intervention. I asked the boy to come over. We spoke a little about his background. My hunch that he was a new arrival was correct; he had been in this country for only eleven months. I assured him that he didn't have to act in a way that didn't feel Afghan. He smiled. We both understood. He removed his cap, returned to his seat, and seemed more relaxed. This was the beginning of a cultural intervention that lasted for the remainder of the year and enabled him to accept both sides of himself, Afghan and American. The process of identifying with his own culture happened first inside the classroom and later outside in the schoolyard.

As I positioned myself in front of the class, the chatter subsided. I began to speak of the year's drama, the possibility of new discoveries for all of us, of hopes, expectations, and limits. Several students slipped out of their seats to find a "translator"—translations were going on, sometimes five languages at one time. I continued to speak. I wanted them to know that we were "in this together." The room was theirs as well as mine. I wanted them to take an active part, not to use me as if I were a television set and they were merely watching. Respect, caring for one another, reverence of differences—all these elements had to be present if we were all going to "make it."

I pointed to the map of the world and asked each of my students to show where he or she had been born. One representative of each country volunteered to come up and point. After the lesson I requested that on the count of three, everyone speak their own language aloud and stop when I rang a little bell. The sounds of linguistic babble and chaos burst forth and then came to a sudden halt as I rang the bell. Dead silence. They waited for the next instruction.

There's a lot of life out there, I thought. I asked the children from each country to pick out a talkative representative to come up to the front of the room. One by one they came up and formed a line. These more articulate ones were not afraid to speak their native languages in front of the group. As each spoke a sentence or two, we listened for the differences in sounds. Together we created our own language. It went something like this: "*Vale ban tôi. Musta ka bine. Si, bien.*" I translated this to mean: "Good morning, I hope you have a good day."

I introduced myself to the class, sharing some of my own multicultural history. I was trying to show them that I understood their backgrounds, but this backfired when, from the back of the room, an arm waved. Another boy from Afghanistan spoke up: "Well, then, you can't help us because we are in America and we have to know English from an American." Again the challenge for intervention.

I explained that yes, they could learn English from me as well as from a native-born American. I assured them that I wasn't a recent arrival and that it had taken many years of study to get where I was academically. Arms began to wave as they questioned my educational background. I went through my second set of interview questions, this time coming from my students and no easier than the ones I had to answer when I applied for the job. When the interview was complete, the group accepted me. They agreed that I would be their teacher and they would be my students.

Setting the Stage

The class and I would have a long uphill climb together. I told them I thought of the year ahead as an adventure in mountain climbing wherein we would be invisibly linked together. As some got closer to the top, they would reach down to help others. Sometimes there would be a slip and someone might slide downhill temporarily, but we would look out for each other and throw a rope. Should someone slip, the others would help him pull himself up toward the summit. All of us would succeed by reaching our highest potentials and facing the academic challenges ahead. The children listened and accepted the challenge. But the responsibility to search for tools to outfit our expedition and the experience to guide it were mine.

I learned that my immigrant students learn quickly if they feel "at home," not only with me but in our room. In Spanish, the saying *Mi casa es tu casa* is a way of inviting people to feel at home, to be themselves while respecting others' needs to be "at home" as well. The message also conveys that the classroom is a serious place for learning. In the classroom, I acted as their guide and also learned from them as they learned from me. Initially some immigrant children are surprised or even skeptical of the concept of teachers as "students"; but it is an important psychological fact that when they do embrace the idea, they value themselves more and are willing to communicate their experiences and enter into dialogues with me. The more I am aware that each comes to the classroom with a valuable cultural history and language, and the more I show interest in who they are and what riches they have brought to this country, the more I can open the door for them to ask questions and seek information about the new environment. This opens the door for their bicultural selves to emerge.

Parents also need to be brought into the children's education. For some parents, a cultural intervention was needed. In my journal I wrote:

> When I asked the children what they would like to do with
> their lives, they quickly mentioned doctor, lawyer, teacher,
> garbage collector, Ninja turtles, and computer experts.
>   Some of the parents have introduced themselves and have
> entrusted their children to me as their "educational parent,"

as they feel they cannot speak English and cannot help their children with their homework. The children, vulnerable as they are, quickly attach themselves to me.

One positive aspect of this bonding is that they are easy to inspire, but without sufficient materials and books, it is difficult to do the work necessary to help make a difference. One motivated boy came to me and asked for extra homework. I had to put him off for three days until I could find materials and books to lend him.

Now that businesses are helping the schools, I wonder if anyone out there could contribute books. The children asked for extra homework but I had no materials or books to give them. I wonder who would be willing to make a contribution to help us with materials, because we need to give these children a fine education.

Building the Nest

Colleagues responded to our needs. Dr. Constance Beutel, a friend and colleague who heads the self-directed education program in a major company, spread the word to managers and staff interested in education. I was asked to speak to them, and I in turn responded. From everywhere people called to offer books and materials. They gathered binders and paper. Members of Dr. Beutel's staff contacted schools that had closed where books, typewriters, earphones, and cassette players were available. Members of church groups also heard our story and responded. We loaded up. Four car loads and a pickup truck! From the point of view of some teachers, the books weren't useful and were obsolete. As I went through them, each book had something useful for expanding vocabulary, cutting out pictures, or offering other meaningful experiences. Even the basal readers and spelling books could be used by some children who needed carefully sequenced language books or extra homework.

The Home Library

With the abundance of books, I encouraged the children to take some home to create their own home libraries. They were energetic, exuberant, and eager to take what I could offer, once I sorted out books that would be helpful. Whether or not they could read the books was not as important as the idea of establishing an interconnected relationship between school and home. There was tangible energy generated by the abundance of books and the children's own stories of how they set up their home libraries.

Home Libraries

Inspired by their enthusiasm, I loaned the children a simple camera to photograph their libraries. They took turns taking the camera home and sharing the pictures with me. For some children this was their first experience owning books and having a library in their own home. In her journal, a girl from Afghanistan wrote:

> *I like having a home library because if I feel like reading, I can read. I didn't have enough books at home, but now my library is full. I didn't have a home library in Afghanistan or India.*
>
> *I got a lot of books from the class. I'm sharing my library with my sister. This morning my sister took a book; she left the book on my bed and I put it back. This weekend I read about 90 pages.*
>
> *Every time when I go to bed, I turn on the lamp and read. I'm practicing how to read. My father thinks the library is good, but not to read at night because of my eyes. And my mom says the same thing. The bed is warm and you feel safe so you start reading.*
>
> *When I go on reading the book, I feel like I am in the story. Once I was reading about a boy running after a puppy, I felt like I was running after the puppy.*
>
> *My father bought me a cabinet for my library and for my*

things. I have my own bedroom and my TV, but I don't usually watch my TV. My father said he would like to read some of my books.

Opening the Door to Dialogue

Shortly after I got acquainted with the entire class, I prepared quiet, productive activities on which the children could work individually or in pairs without my direct participation. I trained two to four mature students to be student teachers who could act as monitors if questions needed answering or directions needed clarification. I gave these student teachers opportunities to take small responsibilities in responding to their peers' needs, such as giving permission to sharpen a pencil or encouragement to the insecure.

What I sensed during the first few days of teaching the entire class was a feeling of collective helplessness and hopelessness. They were exhausted. I was exhausted. As I looked across the room at the global reality of children from all corners of the world, I knew I needed to find out who was there and where they came from so I could prepare the curriculum. As the children worked quietly, I met with each student for a one-on-one dialogue. It was a profoundly rich experience.

At the university level it is often a given for students to meet individually with professors to clarify mutual expectations, discuss academic concerns, and bring up matters that might affect attainment of goals. In our classroom, such dialogues gave the children the opportunity to express themselves; and the dialogues became an important methodology in my working with the students. Through the dialogues I found a way of connecting with each child as a unique individual, validating the child's cultural history, and establishing a trusting, respectful, and warm relationship. As I listened I became aware of areas for CAP intervention. I saw that just a simple word or two could transform a child's attitude and help unblock his or her potential for academic success.

I set up a little "office space" around my desk and met with each student for about 15 minutes. During the dialogue, I inquired into the style of teaching and method of learning used in the child's country of origin. I also wanted to know if the child came from an academically supportive home. If the child wasn't ready to talk with me or needed more time, I scheduled a meeting at a later date in a more private location. If the child confided to me about a troublesome or financially difficult home situation, I expressed concern and told the child that I would make referrals if needed.

I assured the children, especially those from war-torn countries, that they were safe in the classroom. After all, the school was in a difficult neighborhood. I could not assure them that they were safe in the streets, but the one place they could feel free of fear was in the classroom.

For those who preferred to remain silent, I entered the silent stage with them by respecting the child and waiting. If there was resistance, if the child wasn't ready to talk, we spent time together quietly in order to establish trust and warmth. I spoke very directly to the child and tried to find out what I could do to make it safe for the child to speak to me. I felt that if I could figure out what the child was feeling, I could understand his or her behavior.

Validating the Child's Culture

Once I had completed the dialogue with each student and had read up on each child's cultural heritage, we prepared for a celebration. We set a day for the students to bring their native food, music, and costumes, and we invited those who had learned cultural dances to add to the festivities meant to honor cultural differences.

I had to be careful to give equal time for all cultures. The more extroverted children wanted to monopolize the music and made faces at the sounds of music "foreign" to them. They argued among themselves for more time. I expressed some frustration, for I had not expected the "war" to be brought into the "safe" classroom environment; but the fact that they were able to express openly the negative aspects of cultural diversity meant that it was time for cultural intervention. I spoke honestly about similarities and differences and the need to listen attentively to the unfamiliar sounds of the music from other lands and to allow a multicultural classroom to evolve.

Having opened a safe channel for the children to share their inner world with me, and after the celebration of multicultural validation and sharing, I asked the children to write what they could about where they came from and what had brought them to the new land. They worked in groups and assisted one another when language limitations prevented them from writing what they wanted to say. They included drawings of their flags, foods, and costumes. When I asked the children what it meant to them to belong to a cultural group, I received several spontaneous answers ranging from "dances" to "wonderful food" to "religion." In their own way they wrote about their countries and about how they felt. This project took weeks to complete, for there were children who did not know how to trace a map, color a picture, cut and paste, print legibly, or take pride in their work. Integrating lessons in art, reading, writing, and awareness of their own cultural histories took the greater part of each morning.

Multicultural Awareness

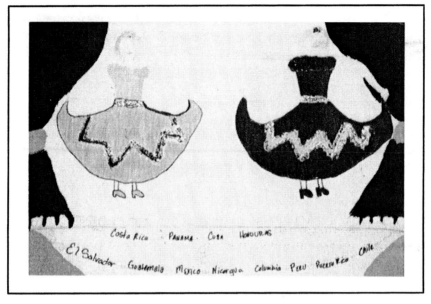

I also showed them how to use tape recorders, which the children took turns bringing home to their families to capture the sounds of their cultures—their languages and music. Engaging their families in this project was one more way of validating their culture and giving each child a connection between home culture and school culture.

The Home–School Connection

After the first couple of months of school, I usually begin to receive invitations from the children to visit their homes. I remain open to visiting those families who wish to have me. It gives me the opportunity to assist the child in finding a connection between home and school.

The importance of the home–school interaction has also been strongly emphasized by Alma Flor Ada in both her practice and her teaching (Ada, 1993). During my visits to the child's home I gain insights on how best to support the child at school and how parents can assist the child at home. Some parents educated abroad entrust their children to the school out of a deep cultural respect for teachers. I, in turn, mediate and encourage their participation in their child's education.

Sometimes, in their enthusiasm that the teacher come to their homes, the children ask when they can come to my home. Children from some countries, like Mexico, share their happiness about having visited their teacher's home before coming to this country. I have some degree of hesitancy about this matter because the intent of the visits is to establish a home–school connection rather than a home–home connection, which for practical reasons would be impossible. For psychological reasons the concern is that some immigrant children do not have their parents in this country. It is possible that these children and those from war-torn countries may become attached to the teacher, when they really need to be attached to their family guardians and peers. The issue is that some children uprooted from their homeland are vulnerable and may, by visiting the teacher's home, develop false expectations—with negative results. In the United States there is also the matter of litigation and lawsuits, should children hurt themselves outside their own homes.

It is best, I think, to keep the focus and energy on the immigrant child's own development in the new country. The home–school connection is important because even though initially it takes conscious effort to help the children bring their cultural heritage out into the open, once they bring it out, they enjoy sharing what their lives were like in their homes. They like bringing meaningful artifacts to school and sharing stories about what they did after school hours. Many of my students have spoken of the games they had played in Romania and in Vietnam, for example, and how they have taught these games to neighborhood children in America. All this has helped generate ideas for developing writing skills through storytelling.

In their homes, when I observed some children make fun of their parents for their inability to read or write, it gave me an opportunity to do some home–school cultural intervention. I spoke with each child in the presence of the parents and showed the child how much I respected the wisdom of the parents and how much he or she could learn from them. I was conscious of preventing the cultural split in the child. I will return to the story of the classroom after some reflection on healing the cultural split.

Parental Involvement in Healing the Cultural Split

My instructional bilingual (Farsi/English) assistant was supportive of these visits and facilitated the parents' trust in me on many occasions. She had two children, was educated in Afghanistan, and lived for some time in Germany before coming to the United States. In every aspect of my work with the children she encouraged bringing their culture out in the open, even preparing assemblies to introduce the schoolchildren to the culture of Afghanistan. Years later I became aware that behind her interest and love of the children was what she called "a mother's point of view":

> *My daughter was seven years old when we came to the United States. The elementary school from first through sixth grade that she went to was a school where there were a lot of students from Afghanistan. She was a straight A student in a GATE [Gifted and Talented] class.*
>
> *When she was in junior high school, there were no Afghan students there. She felt lonely and was very unhappy. Her grades fell from A to B. She wanted to transfer to another school where she could be with students from Afghanistan, but the school district would not allow it.*
>
> *Everybody needs a sense of belonging. When my children came to America they were between the ages of five and seven years old. In school I slowly watched them become Americans to cope with the others. Later on when they were fifteen to seventeen years old they did not know where they belonged. When we celebrated Afghan feasts, they did not feel they could participate. It was at this time that they asked the question, "Who am I?" Because they were not Afghans and they were not Americans. They were confused.*
>
> *They had a conflict. The Americans did not accept them, the Afghans did not accept them. They were in between. They spoke negatively about their culture. They were critical.*
>
> *So we decided to help them. We exposed them to more Afghan feasts and rituals. We took them to Afghan relatives and friends.*
>
> *Now, six years later, they realize that there is some good in their culture. They value our traditions and think positively about being Afghans. It has really helped them have a good self-esteem.*
>
> *Children really need to know that they belong inside a culture; inside a community, because they get support and nourishment from the community.*
>
> RAHIMA ASEFI HAYA

In Part I, Cindy reminded us of the importance of parents in preserving cultural values. I return now to the classroom.

Making a Desk a Home

The room now was decorated with the children's writings, artifacts, and pictures. It had become a nest of familiar and comforting symbols. The children were ready for even more individual expression.

Children's Desks

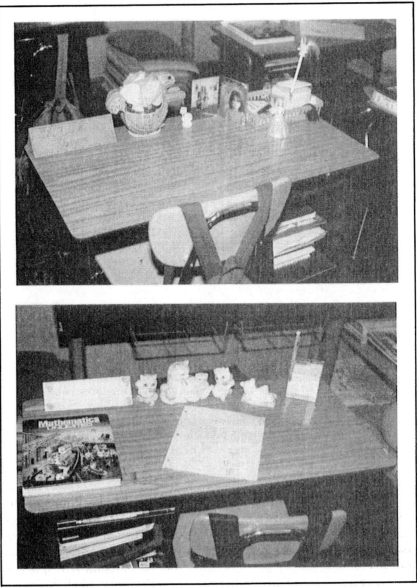

During the dialogic interviews, I found that the children consciously and unconsciously took in everything about me because part of their developmental stage is to mirror an adult whom they respect and who respects them. My desk had a vase with a flower, a pencil holder, and other personal expressions, and soon the children began to bring their own meaningful symbols to create "office space" around their own desks. Some provided decorated trash cans, photographs, or miniatures. When they brought in these articles I was moved, because I knew they were now feeling at home in the classroom.

Once a principal asked if I wasn't concerned that the children might become distracted during lessons and play with the objects on their desks. My response was that I have found that the comfort these artifacts bring to the children actually helps them focus on their work. If the children feel ill at ease, that is when their attention wanders.

Again, I looked to what we adults do to humanize our environment. In business, employees decorate their office space and cubicles with photographs, plants, and souvenirs that give not just pleasure but also a sense of personal identity. Employees who are granted some level of control to feel at home with themselves in the work environment are more industrious and productive than those who are stripped of individuality (Beutel, 1993). If recognizing individual needs in the workplace helps adults work better, why not children? Are not children as human as adults?

Creating Classrooms That Embrace Multiculturalism

In one-on-one communication, it is important to get the children to accept their history and culture and to look forward to beginning to integrate both worlds. I realized that feelings of inadequacy can be internalized by the children from exposure to subtle monolingual/monocultural attitudes implying that one language or one culture is the only way or the best way. In our "nest," each immigrant child learns that the door is open to maintain his or her own language and culture even as he or she learns to live within the new environment.

I speak to the children's inner feelings so that they understand that learning to read in a new language is an extension of what they already know in their own language, and that their life is richer for being able to articulate in more than one way. I encourage flexibility and divergent thinking by presenting the outlook that multiple cultures represent a *both/and* rather than an *either/or* set of choices. I must stress how crucial it is to help the immigrant child cope with pressures to replace rather than supplement his or her native language and culture. The child who responds to unconscious monocultural attitudes is in danger of overidentifying with the new culture and sabotaging his or her own important roots. If immigrant children are not validated to become bilingual and bicultural, if they do not learn to deal with their bilingual and bicultural selves at an early stage, they come to regret the loss of their language and culture later in life.

I recall an 11-year-old Romanian boy who in his eagerness to learn English began to overidentify with the new culture and sabotage his Romanian roots. I honored his insistence but noted it in my journal, so I could observe him closely until I could find an open window to help him embrace his bilingual/bicultural self. I understood that he had observed his father wrestling with the English language in order to find a job in the new country. He felt he needed to learn as much as he could to raise his speaking and reading levels to match his peers, who had come here a year or two before him. He had a sense of curiosity about the United States, the large supermarkets with electronic doors that opened on their own, and the "candies—lots and lots of candies."

→Then his complete identification with the United States and rejection of his past began to express itself as a rejection of classwork. Even his handwriting was careless. Although he did not mind working a little in the classroom to keep up with his peers, he disregarded homework assignments, refused to read or write in his native language, and became playful and talkative in class. When asked what he was to do with his life if he continued to disregard assignments and preferred to spend his school time talking, he reflected for a moment and energetically responded, "Play!" Not only did he need cultural and academic intervention, but he needed parental intervention as well. His father explained that the family had lived in a remote little town in Romania. The school system there was rigorous and traditional. Except for dinner time and a short break with his friends, the boy studied every day from four o'clock in the afternoon until nearly midnight. A sample of his fourth grade homework assignment shows the near-perfect handwriting and the kind of work he was expected to hand in. It was understandable why he wanted to spend the rest of his life playing.

We needed to find a middle ground between the two extremes. The father agreed to work with him at home—both would work together on the assignments. I structured some creative play time where he could work with a friend on spelling games. And I asked the boy to show me the books he had used in Romania. He brought his reading and history books to me, but when asked to read a page of a story in Romanian, he said he had "forgotten" how to read.

Once again I respected his resistance and put the books on a special place on my desk. If he would not honor his roots, I would. The books stayed there until one day, a group of children from Afghanistan asked me to teach them how to speak Spanish. I complied. Soon a group of Spanish-speaking children joined us. Together we were having a wonderful time conversing in Spanish. Out of the corner of

Nicolai's Homework Notebook from Romania

> *18 februarie 1992*
>
> *Problema nr. 2*
>
> *Pe un teren s-au semănat 500 kg de cartofi și s-au cules 5500 kg. De cîte ori s-au cules mai mulți cartofi decît s-au semănat? Cu cîte tone de cartofi s-au cules mai mult decît s-au semănat?.*

my eye, I saw the Romanian boy engrossed in a book. Looking over toward him, I asked, "Nicolai, what are you doing?" He looked up. "Reading the book of my country," he said. At last a window has opened up, I thought. When the group had returned to their seats, I called him over and asked if he would care to read "the book of his country" to me. He read aloud enthusiastically as I listened attentively. Then, pointing to a song in the book, he sang it with much life energy. As Qiu Liang had come alive, so now had Nicolai.

Grief as a Part of Acculturation

Reading "the book of his country" opened up another window, perhaps a door, for Nicolai. Each day as we gathered in small groups he would speak of his homeland whenever relevant. He told the story of how a sudden call from his dad while he was at his grandmother's home totally changed his life. He was told that the immigration papers had been finalized and that he had to come home and pack to go to the United States. He was excited to go but sad because he had to leave his grandmother. He spoke of his grandmother so often that we would have all pitched in to call her long distance, but unfortunately she lived in a remote town in Romania where the telephones were not wired for long distance communication. We encouraged him to write to her and he promised he would. It was important, I thought, that he continue to communicate with his grandmother.

Nicolai was experiencing the grief and loss of the familiar signs and symbols of his native land, and missing his grandmother's warmth. The dialogues seemed to help him get past the grief that is natural to uprooting and helped him begin to accept the transplant to the new country. His open expression of sadness was healthy. He knew that every child in the room understood. He was able to write a poignant little story:

> *Once upon a time there was a very old woman. She was having a dinner with two friends. She went to the store and buy some good food. She called her friends, but there wasn't anybody home. She was real sad. She ate by herself.*

This was a sensitive boy who although curious, talkative, and playful carried a heavy heart. Once he was able to be all of who he was with us, I observed, he began to take more interest in his work.

More than a dozen times the story of Nicolai's grandmother in Romania came up for discussion during the reading lessons. We listened attentively and with genuine interest of his experience gathering chicken eggs with her. How he missed her! She was a significant person in his life, and we included her regularly in discussions to lessen the pain of his loss. Part of him was still in Romania with her and part of him was with us. Toward the end of the year he was more "grounded" in his new country, with his bicultural self emerging. Yet his academic self still was unresolved. In Romania he had had a completely time-consuming academic life during school, after school, and late into the evening. In the United States he still remained on the other extreme, imagining that "play" would become his profession. We continued to talk together and through dialogic intervention hoped he could reach that needed balance. Toward the end of the year, as his peers became serious about schoolwork, so did Nicolai.

Religion as a Part of Culture

A theologian friend and writer (Hart, 1993) once said to me that religion is almost always tied to culture. Henderson (1984) adds that a true religious attitude may become a vehicle for the individual's development. This I found true with the Muslim children from Afghanistan

Mosque

and Pakistan. During the days of preparation for Ramadan Feast, the children fasted with the adults. They were awakened by their parents before dawn. They had breakfast and then went back to sleep until it was time to get themselves ready for school. In school they refrained from food or drink—even a drop of water—until sunset. By noon, especially on warm days, they were a bit listless. I had observed that they refrained from praying in a public school even though public prayer was a part of their cultural attitude. They spoke about their obligation to pray five times daily. In their writing they expressed the conflict within.

> *I always think about my country. I think about going there one day, seeing it and practicing my religion with no problems. Here we don't have enough priests. We call them mullah. Here we have only the mosque. The mullah is important because we learn the Koran from him. I can't practice my religion. Before sunrise, I can pray with my family. But at school we can't say to my teacher, "Please, teacher, I need to pray."*

As the children from Afghanistan began to feel "at home," and with the open communication between us well in place, I was taken by surprise one day while I was lining up the children for school lunch. A group of boys were gathered around the wall map pointing to Afghanistan. Then one ran to the window in search of the direction for Mecca. Another opened cupboards to see where they might keep their prayer rugs, and a third exclaimed, "In Afghanistan it was easy to find Mecca, but we are now on the back side of the globe and we can't find it."

Together they approached me and the "older one" asked if they could pray while the others went off to lunch, as it "would give us a lot of strength." I said yes. It was their choice and not mine to allow expression of that which gave them strength to keep going through the day and keep to their fast. For me their honesty and discipline were inspiring.

When these children shared their cultural heritage with other students in the class during history lessons, their need to pray always came up. As they became comfortable sharing with the others, they would demonstrate how they knelt to pray and what prayer meant to them. The others listened and those with different religious and cultural backgrounds shared and compared, yet at all times they were respectful of each other's beliefs. Religious symbols and the importance of religion often came up in their drawings and writings.

> *Afghanistan religion is very hard, because they have to pray five times a day, and they have to learn the Bible. In our language we are calling the Bible, Koran. Another thing is hard. They have to fast one month. They have to fast from morning to night. They can't eat or drink anything. If they didn't pray five times a day or didn't read the Bible or didn't fast, that means that god wouldn't help them.*
>
> GIRL FROM AFGHANISTAN, AGE 11
> (UNSCHOOLED UNTIL FOURTH GRADE)

> *We have a small mosque where we go on Saturdays between eleven and three. I go to religious school, too. But it is far away. I study Dari and Pashto, the two languages of my country. Then between eight to midnight, I go to the mosque. I believe in Allah and his prophet Mohammed. The Koran is the holy book. There are Islamic rules for everything. Religion is very important in my life.*
>
> BOY FROM AFGHANISTAN, AGE 11

> *The food in school is pork. This is a problem. For example, I just eat pizza because of the cheese, that's all right. Other things I don't eat because I don't know how they make it or if it's not the right way for a Muslim so I do without.*
>
> BOY FROM AFGHANISTAN, AGE 11½

When I spoke to the field supervisor of the school lunches about this, she had already become aware of the Muslim children's food preference and was beginning to remedy the situation.

Homework Notebooks

The children created their own homework notebooks. They cut paper and stapled and designed them. It is easier to purchase a homework notebook, but I prefer a more personal touch. In this book they write their daily assignments. These are signed by the parents, who indicate the time the children took to complete the work. This way I have an idea of how much homework to assign.

Some children like to forge their parents' names, so I usually make a list of the parents' authentic signature(s). This is especially

Homework Assignment

important for the children who have "gotten by" in the system, who have not been accustomed to homework, and who can articulate in English far better than their parents. If the parent can't read English or is not literate in any language, I arrange with the parent that a symbol such as an X mark would indicate to me that the child has studied. I also seek assistance from the student's "buddy" (described more fully on page 141) or from the bilingual teaching assistant to find a way to communicate with the parent directly.

Requiring a parent's signature is a way of including the parents in the education of their children. Moreover, it prevents the children from looking down at their parents for not knowing the language. If I respect the parents, children in turn will respect them.

In the morning as the children enter the room, I quickly stamp their notebooks with a special seal and look to see if there are any messages from the parents. If so, I communicate back to them through the notebook or through a translator—a bilingual teaching assistant. For example, if I cannot speak the language of the parent and there is no translator, usually I ask the child to find me a way. The child often comes up with a workable solution. He or she often suggests an aunt, uncle, relative, or friend to give me a hand on this matter.

Encouraging Peer Bonding

In reflecting upon their immigrant experiences, many of my students have mentioned that the teacher is their closest friend at first and is sometimes the only person to whom they can turn. This was the case with Qiu Liang. However, it is important to encourage peer bonding as well. I often think of Rosario, her long silent stage, and her lack of friends. Peer bonding is a necessary stage of childhood development. Friendships with other children not only ease feelings of isolation and fear but stimulate learning. The learning children acquire through friends is effortless, unconscious, and continuous. Learning becomes a matter of identity, of how we see ourselves (Smith, 1992). Peer bonding is essential because the teacher stays behind when the children move on to another grade, but the peers often move ahead together.

Immigrant children who have achieved second language literacy almost always identify the significance of friends in having helped them adapt to the "new reality." Friends help validate them, act as counselors, stimulate oral language, and even teach reading. In the words of an 11-year-old immigrant girl from Afghanistan:

> *Last year I learned to read and write. The teacher assigned a book and we took it home, but I couldn't speak English. So my*

dad was reading it for me and then explained it. When I went to school I told [my friend] Nadia in Farsi and she explained in English. She helped me read by teaching me the alphabet and how to pronounce the words. And then she gave me easy books to read. I would read them for her and then she gave me harder books and then I could read them. So Nadia was my teacher.

My friends were cheering for me when I did something good. I liked the cheering because it made me proud of me.

Friends are the bridge that will help children cross over to a new class or a new school. The teachers stay behind, but friends move along together. Often when children are engaged in creative activities in class, I try to see if anyone is left out and alone. I do what I can to help that child find a friend by stretching the time of creative activity when I see that the lonely one has begun to connect with another child, or I may ask the child if there is someone he or she would like to work with.

Making friends in a diverse cultural classroom is not always easy because when cultures are so different, it is difficult for a child to find that common ground. One boy from Afghanistan explained:

My family lived in Pakistan during the war with Russia. I found friends easily because we are similar peoples, but when I came here it was more difficult because the people are different.

At first it was boring at school. At recess time everybody was playing. I was thinking I should go back to Pakistan because I have lots of friends there; I thought I would never get a friend in here. In Pakistan I made friends right away.

Today I was happy because my kind teacher let us to play with our friends. She gave us ten minutes to play. My teacher is kind. She help us hard as she could. I hope she will make us very super students.

Play is very important for peer bonding, but I am careful to make sure that the children learn to differentiate between play that recreates and deepens friendships and play that distracts others, gets out of hand, and takes them away from their work. So I structure the time when necessary. I look for ways to help them bond with each other because when they have time to play and can distinguish between play and work, then learning is no longer such an uphill climb. A girl from Afghanistan wrote in her journal:

I'd like to tell you that I enjoy being in class. I like everybody in this class. And this way I learn very fast.

The friends that they establish during play can be very helpful with matters concerning academics. That first year back from "theory to practice," when I stood in front of the class, I felt the children's collective "helplessness"—a draining sort of energy. These were children who had been in the school system for five years, had been in and out of mainstream classrooms, and were still unable to keep up with the others. These same children had also been in sheltered classrooms and still consciously or unconsciously called for me to "solve" their problem. To hear the cry from one child is one thing; to hear it from an entire class is overwhelming. So I decided to share the responsibility and helped them form study groups.

Study Groups

I found I could simultaneously assist with peer bonding and help the students learn by setting up after-school study groups. I first taught the children how to study with each other in the classroom. From my dialogues and some additional research, I determined which children could best study together according to where they lived in the neighborhood. It was best, of course, when the children themselves volunteered to work together. Each study group was designated with the responsibility of obtaining assignments, arranging for study sessions, and seeing that members of the group came to class prepared. An immigrant boy from Afghanistan, age 11, explained:

> It was so easy if you are in a study group. It wasn't hard to spend three hours in the group. I was proud of myself because I want to learn very quickly to get what I want to be.
>
> In my study group we met in a truck. We put rugs in there, and it was a safe place and nobody was bothering us. We just concentrated in the truck. The truck was my brother's. There was room for all of us—it had a roof.
>
> Sometimes in the back of our house was a grassy place and we put a rug there and studied. It was peaceful.
>
> I was the boss of the study group. I said, "Sit down. I'm the oldest." In Afghanistan they have respect for the older one.
>
> We had three dictionaries from our class and each one [of us] looked for one word. And we got the work easily done. For reading time, we all just sat around and each got a turn to read.
>
> It was easy to be in the study group. It helps you a lot. History was hard for me. I tried my best, but I didn't get it. When you put us in a study group, it was very easy.

This was the immigrant boy from Afghanistan who had asked the "kind teacher" to "solve my problems." In the study group he could

Peer Tutoring

call forth the respect of the younger ones and enjoy the cultural attitude of being the older one. Through the study group he found the way to solve his history problems. He was no longer dependent on teacher alone. He actually became the "teacher" he thought he would need to resolve his academic dilemma.

The Buddy System

This is a system I devised based on the strengths of the cultural concept of "older one." In many countries such as Samoa, Afghanistan, and the Philippines respect for the older one is embedded in the culture. In the Philippines, for instance, the term *ate* (pronounced "ah-teh") means "older sister" and *kuya* (pronounced "koo-ya") means "older brother." The young ones are told to obey *kuya*, and they do. Reciprocally, *kuya* or *ate* looks after the welfare of the younger ones. This concept of shared responsibility facilitates parenting.

In every classroom I search for the older ones and for the children who have always been successful academically. The younger ones are given the opportunity to choose an older one. Much in the same way as the "big brother" and "big sister" help their families, the older ones in the classroom keep the younger ones under their wings by checking their homework notebooks, seeing that they are on task, and being available to assist them when needed. This shared responsibility facilitates teaching.

Once, as I was involved with a group reading a story, an academic buddy spotted his young buddy out of his seat disturbing others. Quickly, he left the group and brought the youngster back to work. Academic buddies often keep the more distracted ones under their wing throughout the day. When responsibility for learning is delegated, everyone is involved in the energy it takes to learn.

Responsibility for Learning

Toward the end of the year, the study groups were in place and the parents were communicating through the homework notebooks and stopping by the classroom after school from time to time. The children were feeling successful a little more each day, and they had become more responsible for their learning. Their friendships solidified as they worked together, so much so that a girl from Egypt referred to her friend from Vietnam as her "sister" and a girl from Mexico wrote about her feelings in the class newspaper:

> *My classroom is really nice. We keep our class as if it were our home. We have a big rug in one corner. There are four pillows on it. There is a small rug at the doorway. In my classroom, everybody's desk is really organized.*
>
> *My teacher gives us a lot of work, but it is fun because she helps us do it. We had to do reports on our countries. Everyone did a really nice job.*
>
> *When we work really hard, we have extra recess. In our classroom there are kids from around the world. If you just visit us, you will not want to go.*

We kept all field trips for the end of the year. After the work was done we visited the zoo, strolled in the park, and ran on the beach. The all-inclusive spirit and friendships that had formed through collaborative learning in class and through the study groups made the trips pleasant. There was almost none of the usual peer rivalry for attention. In class, the children could run the classroom without me. We ended the year with resolutions of responsibility. Having focused on the richness and rewards of the opportunity to become bilingual and bicultural, I encouraged them to become active participants in their own education. Each child prepared a written resolution to take individual responsibility for his or her own learning. I had introduced this idea at the beginning of the year. At that time they wrote simple promises, but toward the end of the year their statements demonstrated more maturity. As I helped them, we reflected on these questions:

Is school important?
Who is responsible for your education?
If you have extra time, what can you do with it?
If you do not know or understand something, what can you do?
If you have work to do, what do you do?

For those who responded to the questions with one-word answers, in dialogue I encouraged them to expand their thinking into longer sentences and paragraphs.

When all the resolutions were complete, we mounted each one on colored paper frames and hung them on the classroom wall. Many children took the resolutions seriously and brought them along to the next school. The boy from Romania struggling for a balance in academic matters became more serious about his school and less playful. For children with strong religious backgrounds, their resolutions made schooling more purposeful. A boy from Afghanistan told of his temporary loss of interest in school, but one day his resolution slipped out of his notebook and he resolved to get back on task.

Children's Resolutions

School is very important because when I grow up my study habits would be good. The teacher is important for us, but she is not only the one that helps us. I help myself. Even if I finish all the books, I will still read so I will get stronger in reading. If teacher didn't give us homework, I will make my own homework.
                                    NASEB, FROM AFGHANISTAN, AGE 11

If I have extra time what will I do? I will read a book. If the teacher is busy, I schedule for myself that day.
    I am always responsible for my education. If I don't understand something I will ask friends and if they don't know, I will ask others until someone can explain it to me. All the people should be responsible for their education like me. BE RESPONSIBLE.
                                    ABDUL, FROM AFGHANISTAN, AGE 11

I am responsible for my own learning. When I am absent, I'll call my friend and ask for the homework. Sometimes if I have nothing to do, I'll take a book and read it. I'll never break this promise because I want to learn.
                                    KHATERA, FROM AFGHANISTAN, AGE 11

I will be curious to do my work. If I have a job, I will do it very well. If the teacher speaks, I will listen carefully. If she is busy, I will find another work to do.

MEDORY, FROM THE PHILIPPINES, AGE 11

If I have to turn in an assignment and I have another thing to do that is not important, I will stop and do the important assignment first.

DIEN, FROM VIETNAM, AGE 11

If I play around, I will waste my own time of learning. I will do my work so no one can put me down. School is very important to me.

NAFIZ, FROM FIJI, AGE 10

I have to do my work because I am responsible for my learning. If I have work to do, I have to do it in time. If I don't know something, I will ask my friend and if he doesn't know, I will ask my friends. I am responsible for my learning education.

NICOLAI, FROM ROMANIA, AGE 11

Follow-Up

The following school year, 3 fifth graders from Afghanistan stayed in my program to become sixth graders, and 2 other fifth graders from Mexico moved into a bilingual Spanish class. The remaining 22 sixth graders moved to middle school to begin their seventh grade, or moved out of town.

All the students in the seventh grade middle school, here called Middle School X, were in either the mainstream or the sheltered programs. The decision was made in collaboration with the children, as we discussed their literacy skills. Those who had been in the country the longest and who were able to handle sixth grade reading material moved into the "mainstream." Those who were reading between the fourth and fifth grade levels were placed in the sheltered classes. Generally, the children had a good sense of their own abilities. Those who were unsure of the "unknown" chose to go to sheltered classes, knowing that if they found the class too easy they could request transfer to the "mainstream."

All students in Middle School X traveled from classroom to classroom during the day. Some of the children from my former classroom had their old friendships split up and their study groups disbanded in seventh grade, but they were able to form new alliances. The one difference between the sheltered program in the middle school and the mainstream program was that the learning of content was somewhat slowed down in the sheltered program. For example, science took one year for students in sheltered and only one semester in the "mainstream," but the curriculum was the same for both.

At the end of the first quarter, I contacted 14 students promoted to seventh grade who were in Middle School X. They were energetic and alive in their new school. With exuberance they began to tell me about their grade point averages (GPAs). This was not something I had taught them, but something they had learned in their middle school. Although I believe that grades can and sometimes do get in the way of learning, the reality is that if the school system uses grades to evaluate success in academia then the children show their versatility and respond accordingly.

In many schools throughout the district, children are passed on ready or not. At times school administrators will respond favorably when asked about a student's progress, when in fact the student is barely making an effort and is barely passing. I list the children's GPAs for information purposes and to applaud their enthusiasm. Their report cards showed that their academic scores were between 3.0 and 4.0, and the children said they felt on top of academic matters. For children who had tried to be in mainstream classes but had "failed," this was an unusually high record. Following is a breakdown of these 14 seventh graders.

Girl from Afghanistan	4.0	Girl from Vietnam	3.5
Girl from Egypt	4.0	Girl from Mexico	3.5
Girl from Afghanistan	4.0	Girl from Fiji	3.5
Boy from Afghanistan	4.0	Girl from Fiji	3.3
Boy from Afghanistan	4.0	Girl from Poland	3.3
Girl from Afghanistan	4.0	Boy from Afghanistan	3.0
Boy from Fiji	3.8	Girl from Afghanistan	3.0

They had begun to climb toward the summit of learning in an American school and discovered what it meant to be successful academically and personally.

The two fifth grade students promoted to a bilingual sixth grade classroom were succeeding, and so were the three who remained in my classroom for a second year. One of the children, a boy from Afghanistan, had to be moved suddenly at the end of that quarter to another school district because of the family's need for a better place to live. He was not ready to be placed in the mainstream, and he stopped by for a visit. He reported having difficulty adjusting to the changes because he was now moving from classroom to classroom and having five teachers. He did, however, believe his literacy skills were strong. He returned to visit and to encourage his friends to study.

For such a boy uprooted from his homeland and now from his classmates, schooling became a problem. I will address the issue of mobility difficulties of immigrant children in the next chapter.

Although the children promoted to seventh grade were successful, raising literacy scores in one year is not realistic for most immigrant children because it puts a certain amount of strain on teacher and students alike. Most of these children had been in the country for an average of four years. It would be better for the children to have the time they need. With a program design such as the one described in this chapter, it is more realistic to say that the children could use an average of three and even more years to achieve academic proficiency in English. This time is relative to the amount and type of schooling th ?y received abroad, their age at the time of arrival, and the quality of the instruction they receive. Studies do show that generally, it takes upwards of five years to gain academic proficiency in English (Ada, 1993).

Reflections

Although instructional methodologies are important to second language learners, the real key is to help each child deal with his or her inner world—with the fears and anxieties that block learning. Once the children feel at home in my classroom and have said everything that they have to say—verbally and nonverbally, written or drawn—about who they are and where they have come from, then I know they are ready to listen to me and ready to learn.

If the immigrant child can get over the emotional hurdle of accepting the new culture without rejecting his or her native culture, if the child can free himself or herself from the emotional burdens of loneliness, isolation, fear of ridicule, helplessness, and anxiety, it then becomes very easy to reach and teach the child. These emotional burdens can be held in check through the threefold intervention: cultural/academic/psychological (CAP). The great methodological debates then fade in importance once the child is truly ready to learn.

5

Schoolwork

Today I think I could learn some more words. I talked with my older brother. I used a very good word that he didn't know the meaning. He said, "That is great." I was very happy. I like to learn words and keep a dictionary. I am also really proud of my report about my country. My Mom was so happy, too.

BOY FROM AFGHANISTAN, AGE 12

Academic Intervention

It is not easy to find the balance between the three aspects of cultural/academic/psychological (CAP) intervention. When we are able to do so, then the child can develop a feeling of well-being. In the previous chapter I explained how I set the stage for the children to feel culturally in tune with themselves, to keep the door open for both languages, and to have a feeling of well-being and support. In this chapter my primary focus is on academic intervention and how important it is for the children to feel not only that they are in an academically challenging classroom but that they can *all* achieve.

When an entire class of fifth and sixth graders who have been in the country for one to six years read haltingly at first or second grade level, have difficulty writing simple paragraphs, and are unaware of how words are spelled, then the problem is complex. The problem is no longer "developmental"; academic intervention is necessary.

Teacher as Researcher

The solution to the problem rests in the investigation. Keen observational and listening skills, home visits, dialogic interviews with the children, and even note-taking may be used to investigate the problem. Here are some questions I ask myself:

Were the children schooled or unschooled before they came into the country?

Was their education fragmented?

Was there clear communication between school and home? Are the children caught in the middle, where parents believe that acculturation is the school's responsibility but the school believes it is the parents' responsibility, so that the children play one against the other?

Are the children dependent on the teacher for learning? Do they have any independent learning skills?

Were they in a bilingual program? Was that process interrupted? Were they taught to transfer skills from one language to another?

Did they learn any English abroad?

How much of their own language did they learn, orally and in writing, receptively and productively?

Were the theories and methods recommended by the district misapplied or misinterpreted by those who came before me? Were they taken too literally?

Was there a clear understanding of the cumulative aspect of language—native as well as second language?

What is the status of the parents?

When I was presented with a roomful of immigrant children of seven to eleven different languages and cultures, who had been in the country for one to six years, and when I received a note from a young Afghan boy saying, "teacher, solve my problem," I abandoned the lecture format and adopted a research approach. I decided to find out who the students were. I could no longer teach the class as a cohesive group. It took weeks to set up the classroom like the one I had at the Center (described earlier), where children learned to work independently and cooperatively, so I could work with small groups of students at a table in the back of the room. There I came to know each child and his or her history. After my dialogic interviews with the children, I prepared a chart that summarized each child's educational history. I then prepared a curriculum that would include all the cultures in the room and that would bridge the academic gaps of this particular class.

Included here is a sample of how I graphed the educational background of my students before I prepared the curriculum (see pages 150–151). It was not difficult to collect this data from the class. At the beginning of the year I prepared a clear chart (see "empty" sample); and when I was in dialogue with each student, I asked for his or her educational background. At other times I met the children in small groups and we filled in the information together. Then the children took the charts home and the parents signed for verification. I listed the student's background in one chart and color coded it or used a symbol system.

I began with the traditional lecture format, then assigned work they could do individually or in low whispers in a group. When I could see that they were engaged, I went to the back of the room and worked with small groups. Slowly, I began to increase the amount of

Chart for Gathering Data

Grade	
6	
5	
4	
3	
2	
1	
K	

Educational Background of Students

Grade	Sample Cross-Section of One of My					
6	Calif. District	Calif. District	Calif. District	Calif. District	Calif. District	Calif. District
5	Calif. District	Calif. District	Calif. Outside	Calif. District	Calif. District	Calif. District
4	Calif. District	Calif. District	Calif. Outside	Afghan	Calif. District	Calif. District
3	Calif. District	Calif. District	Calif. Outside	Afghan		Vietnam
2		Canada		Pakistan		Vietnam
1	Vietnam	Canada	Hong Kong			Vietnam
K	Vietnam	Canada				Vietnam
	Anh *Vietnam*	Nazia *Fiji*	Quan *Hong K.*	Jamil *Pakistan*	Bashir *Afghan*	Minh *Vietnam*

(Nazia column note: *moved around—seven schools*)

- no schooling
- educated abroad
- schooled in English-speaking country Canada or Australia
- schooled in America outside district, or another state
- educated in the district

Jamil began school in the 3rd grade. When the family moved to Pakistan, the school placed him in 2nd grade. He returned to Pakistan for 4th grade, was unschooled for the first part of 5th grade, and then was schooled in California for the last part of 5th grade.

time certain students worked independently so I could lengthen the time others worked with me in smaller groups. Only toward the very end of the year, when the children already had learned to work on their own and knew how to seek assistance from their peers or other adults, did I occasionally resume the lecture format, so the children would be able to succeed in school with whatever teaching style was presented to them. That year some of the sources of their academic problems began to unfold. I began to address them as they revealed themselves to me.

Classrooms of Immigrant Students

Nabi	Sima	Rajnet	Sanoa	Razia	Raymunda	Lucia
Calif. District	Calif. District	Calif. District	Calif. District	Calif. District	Calif. District	Calif. District
Calif. District		Calif. District	Calif. District	Calif. District	Calif. District	Calif. District Bilingual
	.	India	Calif. District	Calif. District	Philip-pines	Mexico
		Calif. District	Calif. District	Calif. District	Philip-pines	Mexico
		Calif. District	Calif. District	Calif. District	Philip-pines	Mexico
		Calif. Outside	Calif. District	Calif. District	Philip-pines	Mexico
		Calif. Outside	Calif. District	Calif. District	Philip-pines	Mexico
Nabi	**Sima**	**Rajnet**	**Sanoa**	**Razia**	**Raymunda**	**Lucia**
Afghan	*Afghan*	*India*	*Samoa*	*Afghan*	*Phil.*	*Mexico*

Sources of Academic Problems

Educational Gap

Many of the children's previous teachers had not recognized the fragmentation of their students' education. They assumed that the children had progressed naturally through the grades and that none had skipped a grade.

I obtained the information on the chart through interviews with the children and confirmed the data with the parents. I also requested copies of each child's report cards, which are often retained by the parents, and other data such as homework notebooks and textbooks the children had used in their native country. I found all this information useful. I equated this process to that which a medical doctor follows in gathering information from a new patient.

From the information on the chart, I was surprised to discover the substantial number of gaps and school fragmentation. As I recalled my own fragmented schooling, I recognized the need to close these gaps. As I probed more deeply into the sources of academic problems, I became aware that the lack of communication between one teacher and another and between one school and another hindered the ability of teachers to provide continuity of subject matter.

I also realized that the children's mobility in their early school years generated the educational gaps that contributed greatly to their lack of progress.

The Mobility Factor

The children experienced not only global mobility but also interstate and intraschool mobility.

In my district the entire school rate of family mobility was as high as 58 percent, as families searched for better living conditions and work. Some children in my class had had up to three teachers in one year, as the school enrollment dropped and classes were balanced. One Mexican boy who was small for his age was moved from mainstream to bilingual to sheltered classes in one year. He was finally diagnosed as "special ed." This same boy was "promoted" to my sixth-grade class, skipping a year, because the school administrators were concerned about his age and the social "trouble" he might create in junior high. The boy spent the greater part of that first quarter hiding under his desk, obsessing that he had never completed the fifth grade and wanting to return to his "teacher." Although the age and social issues are a concern for the general population, for many children what is important is that they can handle academia. The school assumed that the child's self-esteem would be raised in my class, failing to see that self-esteem is a by-product of academic achievement and of the child's own feeling of being potent and in charge of his life.

Misunderstanding

Some teachers who had taught my students thought that time would resolve the children's inability to read. They were unaware of the significant gaps in the children's academic education and of the mobility factor.

Some teachers did not understand the silent stage. They waited for the children to speak before they offered them reading books. They were unaware that personality types and cultural values play an important role in the development of literacy. In fact, I have found that many immigrant children who have already learned to read are able to slip right into reading a second language even while in the silent stage. For example, children from Vietnam, China, Poland, and other countries—who received substantial cultural validation through academic achievement in their homeland—learned to read English while in the silent stage; writing followed, and for some, speaking was last. A boy from Fiji commented, "When I first came, I understood everything they were saying. I just couldn't speak."

I found that allowing children to learn a second language in the sequence of skills in which they are ready to learn is more in tune with the culture and personality types of children. The extroverted child will more likely break into speech first, whereas the introverted child will take longer. The former will be able to speak to a group easily, whereas the latter will speak more on a one-to-one basis.

After a week in the classroom, one Vietnamese girl took my hand and with her finger spelled "r - e - d" to show me she was ready to read stories. Within a week she was writing to me in her journal. Speaking came last, as her vocabulary increased through reading, dictionary work, and study groups with Vietnamese classmates.

Jan. 8, 93

I really had a fun the computer room. The first time I so scray. I just know how to type the lettle.

Mar. 8, 93

Last Friday my friend and I did the test, and then I watched T.V. and I do the math. Some hard I don't know I asked the teacher and my friend. And I read language arts.

April 22, 93

An experience I will never forget was when the first day I went to school. That day I was so scared, but I just know how to type a letter in the computer room. When the recess time, I don't want to go outside and play, because I want to stay with my Vietnamese friends. And also I don't know how to speak either. When the teacher want to talk to me, I can't speak. I understand what she said but I don't know how to speak with her.

Some of the children had been treated by their teachers as if their minds were blank slates, because they might have stared blankly when they first arrived. A curriculum had been prepared for them to learn approximately ten words a day. But between the time these children went home each day and the time they sat blankly in class, they were already learning vocabulary through experiences at the supermarket, watching television, in the bus, and so forth. Outside of school, learning was limitless. In school, their learning was dependent on the teacher.

Some teachers correctly expected that the interesting, fun activities of field trips and games would facilitate the learning of a second language. However, some waited too long before giving the children cognitively demanding tasks, putting reading and writing on hold. As they waited for the children to speak, they gave them no homework and reduced their academic responsibilities in school. As a result, there was regression toward infantile behavior. Activities the children would never do abroad, they were doing in the classroom—sword fighting with rulers, disregarding the teacher, walking around the classroom, distracting others, and more. The children assumed a playful attitude toward schoolwork, disregarded and failed to complete homework assignments, and expected that the teachers, who worked diligently preparing materials until late hours, would make the subject matter comprehensible for them. I encountered a few children who had been in the country and in the school district from first grade through fifth grade who were illiterate in both English and their primary language.

One boy from Afghanistan who had started schooling in the first grade in the district entered my sixth grade class with a playful attitude. He was intelligent and articulate and could even pass for being American-born, but he was illiterate in Farsi and English. The task of teaching him how to read and write at such a late date was difficult, and it necessitated academic as well as home interventions. Yet in one year he was able to put his native intelligence to work with the help of his sister at home and the study groups at school. He raised his reading ability up through third grade level. However, the process of speech-print connection could have been started much earlier.

Dependence at School and Home

The belief of some teachers that they are responsible for making all subject matter comprehensible can be problematic if it is taken literally, because the children themselves can come to believe that they do not have to make an effort—teacher will do the work. Children have amazing faculties for making subject matter comprehensible for themselves. If these are tapped, the teacher does not have to overextend herself. After one Vietnamese girl had been in my classroom for three days, I asked her to please bring me an eraser and I pointed to the chalkboard. All the children immediately responded, "She doesn't understand English." I waited. The child went quickly and returned with the eraser. There is a lot that goes on in the silent stage. Beyond our comprehension, they comprehend.

One mother explained that she had done everything for her child—feed, wash, and cook—because the child was without a father for four years while he went ahead to the United States to find work and a place to live. She wanted the boy to feel loved and she wanted to be close to the boy. I understood the mother and became more aware that at school I needed to help him begin to do things for himself.

Another young girl had been told by her mother that at the age of 17 she would be married and could depend on her husband to take care of her. This complexity of cultural gender-role expectation was one I understood well, having grown up in the islands. The youngster finally did begin to read. As she watched her peers progress in literacy, she brought her reading books home to study. On graduation day I was reprimanded by her mother because the daughter had studied until late hours of the night, but the father winked at me knowingly.

After examining all the sources of the children's academic problems, I preferred to work with the children in small groups while the rest of the class worked independently. It took from September to December to get the children acclimated to this approach and for them to take responsibility for their schoolwork. Now that the problems had been diagnosed, educational tools and techniques could be put to work.

Adapting the Traditional Approach

All the children who came from traditional schools abroad were comfortable and learned quickly when I used some traditional approaches. "At last," said one boy from Ukraine, "I feel I am in school, I feel like a student." In their drawings the children depicted what their classrooms looked like abroad. Schooling for many in their native country was a formal experience. They told of teachers "hitting (their) hands with rulers" if they misbehaved or failed to do schoolwork. Fun, games, chatter, and laughter were unheard of for some. They were confused by the American way and misunderstood fun activities as "wasting time." I compromised by changing the arrangement of their desks from straight rows of individual desks to straight rows *in pairs* to foster friendships. Then gradually, toward the end of the year when they could work independently, I arranged their desks into co-

Classroom in Afghanistan

operative learning tables. At all times I was refocusing the children
from a teacher-centered approach to a student-centered approach
whereby the children assigned themselves homework in collaboration with me, prepared their own afternoon schedules, evaluated
their progress, kept their work in their own folders, and gave input
about their report card grades. In this way they made a gradual
transition from their classrooms abroad to their new classrooms as
they participated in their own learning and planning.

Schedule of the Day

As part of my teaching practice, I schedule the subject matter
content on the board as "work of the day" and allow time for the
children to reflect on their own academic strengths and weaknesses.
They write themselves a list of things to do when the assigned work is
complete. If a child writes down that she will work on her multiplication tables, I ask her to be more specific. She might say, "I do not
know my 8X (multiplication) table." The child soon is able to pin-
point math areas in which she is weak. I survey the room until everyone has a "Post-it" note attached to their "office desk" and I approve
their personal assignments. I then move to the back of the room and
work with small groups. As they learn to assign their own schoolwork, at times I allow them to schedule an entire afternoon. Most
children schedule unfinished work that I would have scheduled myself. Because they are at all levels of the academic spectrum, they
know best what is left unfinished.

A Child's Schedule

```
-Watch the movie                              □
· 12:00  to  12:15  read  scolastic News □
· 12:15 to 1:00 Lunch and resses .  □
1:00 to 1:30 practice handwriting  □
1:30 to 2:00 do  dictionary words  □
2:00 to 2:30  read a book  □
2:30 to 2:45 write  down homework
and chat a little and go home.        □
```

The Lesson Plan

Working with these children, I plan the lessons on a daily basis rather than on a weekly basis, because it is important to continue each day from where I left off the previous day. In this way the children do not feel like the Vietnamese girl, Dung, who said that just as she was beginning to understand, the teacher moved on in the lesson, leaving her behind, frustrated and anxious (see Chapter 3). By taking a day at a time, the children do not have to feel rushed and I can ensure that everyone "gets it." I do find this plan works.

I also schedule time for home visits after school, which I have discussed previously. I will touch on this again later. It is not as time-consuming as one may think, and it has a good payback in the long run.

Content Areas

Literacy

The entire morning is dedicated to the development of strong literacy skills—reading, writing, spelling—and numeracy. I usually disregard the school bells and run right through the greater part of the morning until every child has had a chance to read to me one story a day. They go over that same story for homework with their study groups. I then increase the assignment to one story a day, one story at night.

The first readers introduce the children to one-word sentences, then longer sentences with a comma, then sentences with adjectives, and verbs, and so on cumulatively. As we read and discuss the stories together, we look at the punctuation and discuss the language style as well. Then they reflect on their own lives and share personal experiences with the group. Sometimes it is in response to something they have just read; sometimes it is because a child has been reminded by the reading of an experience in his or her home country and wants to share with the group. Then we take time to talk about the structure of the language. They give input as to how their language is different from English. A Romanian boy may remind another about the letter *k* being silent in "know." Because the tone of trust is set, we'll all help the Filipino boy with the sound of *f* because that letter is not in the Filipino alphabet, and we'll all help the girl from Nicaragua with the difference between *ch* and *sh*.

Because the children are taught to observe the language carefully, each day they select a page from the story for spelling dictation. I believe that they need to see and experience their gradual linguistic growth to overcome their "helpless, hopeless" feeling. We then correct the work together. Those who need to "observe" again review with a friend and take a spelling dictation re-test on the same day. Some ask to take the work home. We then fill up a wall space with every child's excellent work. The children are enthusiastic about a daily test of their written language growth through these daily dictations, because they receive immediate feedback on their progress and a chance to re-test for mastery.

Three strengths are in their favor: the fact that many of the schools in their native countries taught them the art of memorization; the fact that many believe that if they put in enough time and effort they will succeed; and the fact that they arrive with curious minds.

Having been "observers of life" during the silent stage, the children are very capable of observing the written word and making comparisons. For example, they are able to see that three small words are contained in "together": *to-get-her*. With practice, spelling becomes easier for them. Some become so enthusiastic about spelling that they carry their enthusiasm to their after-school karate classes— "spell 'black belt'" and so on. At the end of the year, one Egyptian girl walked around the classroom on graduation day exclaiming, "Test me, test me. I can spell anything." With spelling strengthened, their writing becomes easier to read.

I have observed that some Spanish-speaking children who are used to spelling easily in Spanish are disappointed to find it difficult to spell in English. But when they phoneticize the English word in the same way they learned to do in Spanish, then it no longer is a problem. For example, the children take the word *beautiful* and sound it out in Spanish: (bĕ)(ah)(oo)(tĭ)(foōl). Then they write the word as they hear it in Spanish. This way they can remember all the vowels in the English word.

I find that all the immigrant children—especially those from Vietnam, China, Afghanistan, Egypt, and India, whose reading and writing forms differ from English—are successful in learning a second language through this approach to literacy.

Those who have skipped a year or more of schooling, however, find comfort in the basal approach to reading, whereby the amount of words to be learned increases gradually in a systematic way. Each page of the book adds a few new vocabulary words rather than overwhelming the child (who, for example, may be crossing over from Farsi to English) with too many new words at a time. It is also a sound approach for the unschooled child who wants to feel that he or she, too, can read. To get a sense of literature, these children also listen to stories from children's literature or sit in with as many reading groups as they wish. They join in discussions after listening to stories read aloud and transfer skills learned in the basal readers to their literature stories when they are ready.

To be unable to read is to be powerless; in the children's words, "helpless, hopeless." Says Dung, it is to fear that "I will never make it" in school or in the world. I work with the children until the energy in the room is kinesthetic and the children are alive and reading; until they can say or write what the two following children have written in their journals. The first goes right into reading. The second transforms a boring weekend into an interesting one through reading.

> *Yesterday, I went home, I did my homework. First thing I did was read. It was kind of hard, but I got the idea.*
> GIRL FROM MEXICO, AGE 10

> *This was the most boring weekend I've ever had because I was at my grandma's house and my cousins wouldn't stop watching their programs. I enjoyed nothing. But there is one thing that I liked. Reading.*
> GIRL FROM AFGHANISTAN, AGE 11

I do not get into endless debates as to which is the best approach to helping children gain English literacy. I follow my instincts, fall back on experience and methods that have worked for me, and observe the children, because I do not believe that there is one method that works for all children, all cultures, all the time. It is best to use a combination of methods. I meet them along the road to literacy wherever I may find them. We walk together to find ways to reach their fullest potential.

These children have dreams, and they need to be literate to achieve them. When their dreams manifest themselves in their journals, then I know they feel motivated.

> *I wish that I could go study at University. I hope my wish will come true. When I grow up, I want to be a nurse, that's why I want to go to University.*
>
>   GIRL FROM FIJI, AGE 10

> *I wish I could pass every grade I go to and be the smartest kid in school.*
>
>   GIRL FROM AFGHANISTAN, AGE 11

> *I wish that I was in twelfth grade and I was getting better and better so I go to college.*
>
>   GIRL FROM MEXICO, AGE 10

> *I wish I was a movie star, because I want to be the first Afghan girl who is a movie star in America. I want to be famous.*
>
>   GIRL FROM AFGHANISTAN, AGE 11

The dictionary. After going over the use of a dictionary, the children make their own dictionary books where they collect words from the stories. Vocabulary expansion is important. The skill of looking up a word themselves gets them out of their sense of helplessness. They either look up the words, illustrate them, or write the meanings in their own languages. When they understand the meaning of the words looked up, they try to use them or incorporate them in their writing or in their jounals. I encourage them to use the words in paragraphs. Where their vocabulary is still expanding in their writing, I act as a "walking dictionary," giving them the word they search for as they write. I move about the room rather quickly as they raise their hands for my attention. I enjoy these moments, for it becomes a game of how fast I can get to them and how fast they can write. They get so good at looking up words that sometimes I ask aloud, "What does this word mean?" Hands begin to raise quickly. Some search their desks for their dictionaries and a few run to the back of the room to search for the word in the larger collegiate dictionaries. Words. How important they are for communication.

Page from a Child's Dictonary

VOCABULARY
AND
PICTURES
by: Fernando Cordero
1. Mackintosh - A raincoat.

2. Whirl - To revolve or turn rapidly

3. Pleased - Giving pleasure; to be agreeable.

4. Blade - A leaf of grass.

5. Odd - Strange.

6. Slumber - To go into deep sleep.

7. Meadow - A piece of grassy land.

8. Brook - A small stream.

9. Hoot - The cry of an owl.

10. Daze - To stun or confuse as by a blow.

11. Dipper - A cup-shaped container having a long straight handle, use for scooping up liquids

12. Flock - A group of animals of one kind.

First language. I reserve the last period of the day for the children to listen or to read in their own languages. Three times a week, college students who speak their languages will assist. (This happens only when the college students are available.) It keeps the children interested in their primary languages.

Many children from "mainstream" classes want to join in these classes, and flexible teachers allow them to take the class in Farsi, Vietnamese, Spanish, or another language of their choice. This is a wonderful experience for the immigrant and the "mainstream" child alike. Both groups of children have written about it as a positive experience in school.

> Tôi sống trong 1 gia đình bình thường mọi
> người rất thương tôi lo cho tôi đi học, tôi
> học tôi lớp 4 tôi nghỉ học tôi rất buồn.
> Và sau đó me tôi lo cho gia đình đi qua
> mỹ để cho tương lai chị em tôi được sáng
> ngời, và gia đình tôi đi qua phi để học, bên
> phi tôi ráng học để được me tôi trong ước
> nguyện, tôi học ở phi được 6 thang và cuối
> sống bên phi vật khổ và hay đụng trạm.
> và sau đó gia đình tôi lại qua mỹ đinh cư và ở
> với ông bà, không bao lâu tôi lại đi học, và tôi nghỉ tới
> tôi ước mong của mà tôi ở biết ra sao. và
> tôi cũng ở làm cho mà tôi thất vọng.

I live in a middle class family. Everyone loves me very much. They sent me to school to study. I went to school until I was in the 4th grade, then I stopped going to school. I was very sad. After that, my mother helped my family to come to the U.S. for a better future.

My family travelled to the Philippines. In the Philippines we learned English, I studied very hard in order to make my mother happy. In the Philippines I went to school for 6 months. The life there was very difficult for us. After that my family went to the U.S. where we lived with my grandparents. I go to school here. I do not know what are my mother's hopes and I also do not want to disappoint her.

TRANSLATED FROM VIETNAMESE

For the immigrant, here is also a chance to shine in the language he or she developed and an opportunity to express his or her thoughts and feelings. The "mainstream" child in these classes realizes that the immigrant is indeed a peer and becomes more accustomed to listening to the sounds of other languages. An example of a child's writing that was shared in this manner is reproduced above.

Numeracy

For numbers, I teach one concept at a time. I do not move on until everyone in the room has understood, because I often recall Rosario's message, "Give me what I can do, not what I cannot do and if I can't, help me." I maintain the philosophy of "we are in this together." It is fascinating to watch how the children help each other and some even spontaneously do last-minute coaching of another student before a test. The message I try to convey is that we are all intelligent and that it may take longer for some to understand a concept, so we give them the time they need. I also encourage the children to ask for assistance from some-one, be it a friend, uncle, aunt, or cousin, if they do not understand.

When I present a lesson in numeracy I wait until all the children are listening attentively. I ring a little ceramic bell to draw their attention so I do not have to raise my voice. The children have been taught to stop at the sound of this bell. I try not to make the mistake of speaking while they are talking. I try to monitor the tone of my voice so they can hear me speaking *to* them rather than *at* them.

I then present the concept on the board first. When eight to ten children understand, I give each of these students a chance at the board to show that they do. When they "pass" they pick two to three students to "teach." With children, this has to be done carefully so the noise level in the room does not become unbearable. As one group gets ready to work, the others wait. I take the time necessary to watch until they are settled and engaged. Then the next group moves. The "student-teacher" takes the group to their "office desks" or to a com-fortable place in the room.

While they are engaged, I go to a table in the back of the room to work with students who need careful attention. Those who finish early return to their desks and begin to work on an art project. Most often they draw or sketch a piece of artwork. This gives me time to see that all have understood the concept. For those who are visual learn-ers, for those who need manipulatives, I go over the lesson with them right there and then. For those who need more support, I call for the study group. I instruct the study group. Sometimes I write a note to the parents so the child can get help at home. This is just one of the many ways I teach this subject.

Science

The children, on independent study once again, search libraries to find hands-on science experiments and projects for oral presenta-tions. They carry out the experiments either individually or with a friend, at school or at home. I have seen the children outside their homes experimenting with balloons and testing out experiments, while in one case a mother from Afghanistan watched. In this way the children are free to test out how well they can read.

Art

Art is fundamental in my work with immigrant children. From the first week until the very last day, the children use their observational ability to draw, sketch, print, or design cultural patterns. Every child learns to draw. The children start with simple sketches and progress to more advanced ones. By the end of the year I can see how their confi-dence and self-esteem have increased as they develop this skill. I also

combine their ideas with those of professional artists who have illustrated their literature books and help them develop their own style. As
they become skilled in art, they begin to draw things that have meaning to them or that give them a sense of their history—for example,
artifacts, mandalas. Things that remind them of home are an important component of immigrant children's artwork, whether they reflect
positive or negative experiences. After a short time, even war symbols
and tanks enter some of the children's drawings (some examples are
included later in this book; see pages 182–183).

Music

The children in my classes learn to appreciate music from all the
countries represented in the room. Because the other schoolwork can
be tedious, I allow them from time to time to listen to cultural music
without voices, or classical music, while they are practicing their
handwriting or quietly reading a book. Sometimes we have a contest.
I plan a time when they bring music from their countries. First, I give
them a few minutes to listen to the music of the various countries,
then the children identify each country in writing. The winner is
applauded and receives a certificate. It is interesting that the most
silent introvert almost always wins.

Classical music is my passion. On one occasion, the room was
very still with minds busy at work. I stopped to take a break and
played one of Chopin's nocturnes very quietly on the piano. As I was
involved in the music, many children slipped out of their seats to
listen and observe. When I finished the piece, the children applauded.
This was my first concert experience, with a most appreciative audi-
ence. After the brief break, we were back on task. Perhaps the lesson
of the moment was that we are all learners—they in language, I in
music. The next day in his personal journal, a boy from Samoa wrote:

> *Yesterday, I decided to take piano lessons. I asked my mom and
> she said it was fine. I think I will start next week at the club.*

I couldn't help but reflect on how interconnected we are in the
classroom and how closely the children observe us.

Issues

Bridging the Academic Gap

Having worked with Qiu Liang (see Part I), providing him a plan
to deal with his feelings, helping him to own his cultural identity and
succeed in academia, I began to apply what I had learned from that

experience to twenty-six other immigrant students in one classroom. This was more difficult, because I was writing the curriculum as I observed the children, listening to their academic needs and balancing the need for cultural preservation. I also realized that with Qiu Liang there was time—two years. With the twenty-six students, there was only one year and there would *not* be continuity the following year. I took into consideration the mobility factor and created an accelerated program.

I put all State Framework curriculum on hold until the children had advanced in language arts first—reading, writing, spelling—and numeracy. I took all the skills a child would normally learn in first grade and made sure the children mastered them alone or in study groups. I gradually moved them up the grades; it took approximately two months for each grade level. We worked all morning until noon, disregarding school bells or set schedules. We would drop what we were doing only for recess and lunch and then return to the task at hand. The children left for recess on their own without having to line up. It called forth a sense of responsibility in them and I did not have to stop what I was doing with a group or individual. All the children went through this process of learning all the skills from ground up— first grade onward. Those who had been in the country the longest were strengthened in every area and were surprised to find that what they thought they knew, they did not. In reading, for instance, many ran right through commas and other punctuation marks, losing the concepts and ideas presented on the printed page. So they learned to slow down for comprehension, to ask questions, and to apply what they were reading to their lives.

The traditional approach of guaranteeing a set number of minutes for each subject, so that a teacher is mandated to change when the bell rings at 45-minute intervals, was very disruptive to the process. The subject change came naturally when all the children had absorbed and mastered a particular lesson or skill and were ready to move on. Those who learned quickly stopped to help the others or moved on to a task written on the "Post-it" list on their desks.

Regarding the use of dictionary skills, I noticed that one child from a remote region of the Philippines did not know how to alphabetize. It took me 45 minutes to show her how while the others were occupied, but once she got it, she was off and running back to her "office desk."

In the afternoon, I alternated between science, history, and finishing up the morning's work. The children also began to prepare reports on their countries for history. They began by sharing stories, making maps, and preparing to write about their countries. The final report booklet was completed by the end of the year when their reading and writing skills had developed.

Progress

By the end of January, almost all the children were reading at third grade level comfortably, quickly, and without hesitation. Once they had said what they needed to say about their countries, I brought in American history books written at the third grade level. Slowly the transfer of skills from reading literature to reading history began to take place. We discussed how to look at history with a critical mind and to see it as an extension of storytelling. I also began to bring in articles from the newspapers for them to read and to report on. As they became comfortable with reading history and as the study groups became well established, I periodically brought in science books they could read and showed them how to transfer reading skills to science reading. Their vocabulary notebooks expanded gradually. The children tested out their new words with friends and relatives.

By March and April, the children were developing fourth grade skills. By May they were beginning to do some fifth grade work. End-of-the-year school activities interrupted the process, so I took key stories from fifth and sixth grade literature books to show the children that they could handle the work with their skills, foundation, and ability. Many took work home for the summer months.

The chart on the next page shows the accelerated academic intervention program that was needed for the fifth and sixth grade immigrant students to bridge their academic gaps and lack of reading skills. I have used this plan successfully in succeeding years, adapting it to each new set of immigrant children. The few in the fifth grade who stayed for two years were able to move right into the mainstream with strong academic skills and a strong sense of cultural identity.

The chart shows the academic plan contained within the boundaries of cultural awareness and cultural acceptance. Both are contained in an environment that is psychologically safe for learning. The intervention plan was designed for children who had been in the country from one to six years. Depending on mobility factors and educational gaps, some children may be able to use this plan for two or more years and should not be "pushed ahead" until they have mastered each level.

The Unschooled or Partially Schooled

The issue of the unschooled or partially schooled child is a separate issue beyond the scope of this book. Three of the children I encountered who were unschooled for between three and five years requested "retention." They chose to stay for an added year and their parents agreed. Because the plan allows children to learn cumulatively, the unschooled children felt successful during both years.

Closing the Gaps

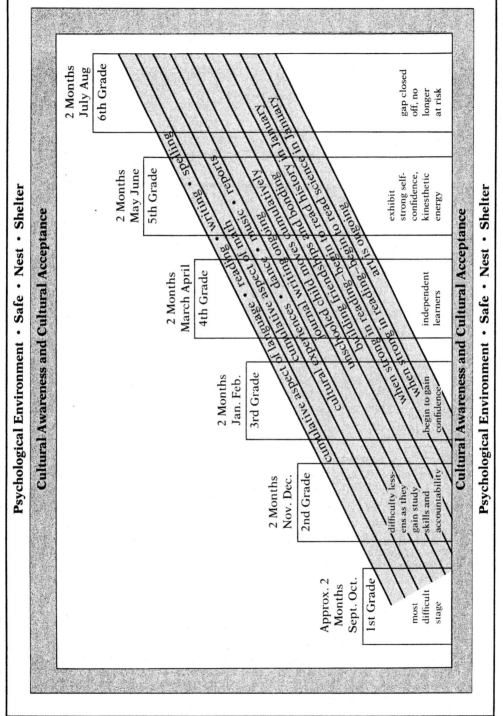

These children need the continuity that the program provides, and they will be "at risk" until all the gaps have been closed. Their success in school also depends on their own commitments, supported by their parents and the amount of schoolwork they can handle after school hours, because the system is not set up specifically for them.

In spite of the uphill climb, one disciplined Afghan girl was able to go up the cumulative ladder and was almost at grade level in reading when the year ended. She took it upon herself to study "all day and all night," many long hours, for she had missed the first three years of schooling. When I visited her home to speak to her family about her overzealousness, they invited me in for tea. The child and the parents did not object to the long homework hours imposed by the girl herself because she wanted to be successful in school. The family lived in close quarters and the younger girls stayed home after school. The only recreation for them was to read, chat, or watch television. This girl chose to read. She became a better reader than her older sister in the eighth grade and helped her with her homework, reversing the roles— "younger one" helping "older one." This was not a problem, however, until the siblings began to tease her. I intervened by discussing the cultural aspects of the matter with the family.

The concept of the "Little Red Schoolhouse" where one teacher stays with the children until they complete all grade levels is what these children need, and some schools are beginning to adopt the model of allowing children to stay with their teacher for three years consecutively. Totally unschooled children really need to stay for a few years with one teacher in an ungraded program. Sometimes I have to make difficult decisions because the system pushes them on before they are ready.

One difficult decision I had to make was the case of an unschooled 10-year-old girl from Afghanistan, who had lived in refugee camps and had never been socialized in a classroom. She littered paper, removed her shoes in class, and glued her name card to her desk instead of using masking tape. I wondered how to proceed besides helping her to adjust in the classroom. For me, even where to begin linguistically was an issue. In one journal entry, I wrote:

> She needs parents to read her stories, but she does not have them. Her mother cannot read or write either English or Farsi. Her father wasn't home when I visited. Six children. Seventh on the way. She is the oldest one. She is probably the one who takes charge at home because in the classroom she is always offering to help, "Can I help you? Can I help you? I will vacuum the rug."
>
> Because of her age, lack of schooling, and different alphabet forms, there is no time to have her start in Farsi and then

shift over to English. I only have one year with her before the
school system will move her along, ready or not. I think
what's important is that she learn to read right away.

Farsi goes from right to left and English from left to
right. With twenty-six other students, will I have time to
teach her to read? Do I make the decision for her to learn
Farsi first or English first, or does her father? Must the decision be made on the basis of life survival or from the theory
handed to us by the district that one "learns a second language through the medium of the first"? But she can't read at
all in any language.

After consulting my journal, I visited her home. Her father
seemed desperate. He was struggling to learn English from a dictionary so he could find a job. He wanted her to learn English, too, so she
could help the family. I decided to move her into English and kept the
door open for her to learn Farsi in time. When I visited her home a
third time, she was thrilled. She jumped up and down and said, "I can
read. I can read, 'Where is the garbage? Where is the baby?' " I then
decided that soon, with the bilingual assistant assigned to my class, I
would teach her to read a sentence or two in Farsi. I wondered if that
would give her even more joy, because then she would be able not
only to speak her native language, but read it as well. Ultimately, this
child took the greater part of a year to get acclimated to a classroom
and another year to begin to read first grade materials. She is intelligent and needs many years with one teacher.

The Personal Journal

My journal is the place where I wrestle with making decisions that
are in the best interest of the students. Sometimes I have to risk going
beyond measured objectives to find the best approach for an individual child, to work through mere subjectivity. It is in the journal that I
clarify my thinking, write observations, and make decisions.

The children also keep personal journals. They write to me to
share their everyday lives, or they write about school. It is where they,
too, can remain in touch with their true selves. It is where they share
their feelings and thoughts with me and where I am able to communicate with them personally.

Student–Teacher Ratio

It is erroneous to think that we can teach a classroom of immigrant children with numerous languages, gaps in education, and
many unschooled all in one room and not consider the importance of

student–teacher ratio. In the first year that the district decided to "shelter" the children, they were placed in the classroom in numbers equal to that of "mainstream" classrooms: 33 to 35 students per class. It was an impossible task for the teacher to reach them all, even with a part-time bilingual instructional assistant. It is no wonder that many children could not develop literacy skills.

With the hiring of another teacher, the student–teacher ratio dropped to 27 students per teacher and at times 22 to 24. This was more realistic. But with a number of unschooled or partially schooled children in the classroom, the total number of students should be lowered even more. It is also important to consider how long the children have been in the country and whether or not they have come out of the silent stage in order to determine the optimal student–teacher ratio.

Home–School Connection

Once again I mention briefly the importance of home–school connection.

Children from extended families find it easy to invite the teacher to their homes for dinner. They treat the teacher as an extended family member—or, as in Afghan cultures, the "mullah," the priest who stops to visit. They recount stories of their lives in their native countries and share their native foods. I use this time to relate to the family how best they can help their child in school.

A short visit after school can be well worth the extra time. In one case I convinced a father from Fiji to spend time with his son, who had fallen behind academically, when I tested the boy after dinner at the table. With the father's support, the boy's reading, writing, and math skills improved. In another case I discovered that a preliterate boy from Afghanistan in my sixth grade class was spending the greater part of the afternoon and evening watching television. He was an articulate, intelligent boy who knew that both parents were unable to speak or write English. With the help of a student translator, I communicated to the father that his signature X would indicate to me that his son had done his homework. The parent agreed and I had a way of knowing whether or not my student was studying at home. Clearly, these home visits bring some startling experiences.

Once I visited a Muslim boy's family after the death of a young relative to console the mother. As I entered the room, twenty women, dressed in black, were sitting around the living room and dining room floor, wailing. The love and feeling of family and community were profound. Family members had flown in from all over the nation to comfort the family. I was moved deeply by this experience.

Positive Values Brought by Immigrants

Working with immigrant children and their families has confirmed my belief that some of their rich heritage and values are needed in America today. I believe it is important to preserve these values within the children themselves, because they will make a difference in our world; they are a part of American history in the making.

I have been awed by their motivation, willingness to take risks, and global vision. They have traveled the world and expanded their own worlds at a most impressionable age. Their minds are flexible, and they are able to see both sides of a situation—over here, it is done this way; abroad, it is done that way. This outlook fosters creativity, a non-judgmental attitude, and an acceptance of reality. I watched an Afghan boy take a book and instinctively open it from left to right. He paused a moment, his mind examining the situation, then flipped the book over to open it from right to left and began to read. It took time, but in that brief moment of thought he was developing his reflective nature and his ability to take in two worlds.

I have been touched by the parents' generosity and their respect for a teacher who in their minds embodies the one who "sets the child on the way or path to develop intellectually and spiritually to achieve

a goal in life" (translated from an Old World dictionary). Several times, I have been surprised to see a mother from Afghanistan in native dress standing at my classroom door as the children were dismissed for the day, holding a tray of food for my dinner; or a mother from El Salvador stopping by to give thanks.

I appreciate their warmth, hospitality, love of family and children. I respect the all-inclusive nature of their extended family concept. When I visited a family from Fiji once, I saw an elderly man sitting comfortably in the family room watching television, enjoying himself with the children. "Teacher," said the mother, "my husband works as manager of McDonald's and this man has no family. He eats at McDonald's every night. So, we ask him to come visit us. He is like our grandfather."

In general, these immigrants are rich in artistic expression, rich in rituals, rich in music and dance, and have a great respect for education. They have an innate ability to celebrate life and to include others in their celebrations. When their resources are tapped, then indeed, I think, we will have discovered the "gold" we have been seeking.

Reflections

How important it is for teachers to become critical thinkers who are research-oriented. As we understand research done by others and examine all variables, we need to do our own research in the classroom so that we use theories to guide us rather than reducing them to formulas to be followed blindly. To follow theories as formulas would be a mistake.

Immigrant children come to us with their own experiences. We must become observers of life in our own classrooms. Our curriculum and school subjects must be as alive, challenging, and ever-changing as the children are.

There must be subject-matter continuity and an understanding of the cumulative aspect of language. Literacy must be high on the teacher's priority list because without the ability to read, children feel disempowered. We need to examine all subject areas for cultural biases and look within ourselves to examine our own cultural biases.

While the children learn from us to be true to their own culture and to appreciate one another's culture, the academic work needs to stay clearly focused and balanced between the cultural and psychological.

6

Cultural Continuity

I enjoy being in this class. Everybody understands me and
with students from around the world, I can learn about
Afghanistan, Fiji, Pakistan, Mexico, Salvador, Guatemala, and
other places. It is interesting to learn about other people and to
meet new people, too.

GIRL FROM EGYPT, AGE 11

Cultural continuity, cultural cooperation, and understanding of each other's differences is what this Egyptian girl is talking about. It means finding the common bond between people that makes learning enjoyable and more interesting, she says. Yet cultural discontinuity has been evident in many of our schools (Trueba, 1993) and dates back to the beginning of U.S. colonization; the first attempt at cultural change was in 1830. For example, at that time the Native Americans were removed from the southeastern part of the United States and placed in Indian Territory. The children of these Native Americans were taken from their families and tribes and placed in non-reservation boarding schools (Spring, 1994). Only after the Native American cultures were systematically destroyed has there been a realization that the opportunity to learn what they had to teach was also lost. Now, students study their values and ways of life. From a distance we study their lifestyles, create teepees and headdresses, and talk about Native Americans in our classrooms. We also learn about African Americans, Puerto Ricans, Mexican Americans, Central Americans, and Asian Americans who have been forcibly subjected to cultural discontinuity.

If it is possible to learn from past mistakes, perhaps we can begin with the immigrant children to "heal our society" and to develop in all children "peace, harmony, respect for cultural differences and co-operation towards common goals" (Trueba, 1993, p. 140). This can be done through the influence of teachers (p. 137). I believe our task is profound, but we teachers can contribute to a more peaceful America, beginning in our classrooms in our own small way. What children learn in one year can carry them through a lifetime—every year is important in the lives of children. There are many ways we can foster their cultural continuity; one way I like to do it is by the report format, which, when finished, can look like a book that tells their story.

Reports about Native Country

An old method, a new purpose. Part of one of the major components of curriculum for the immigrant children I work with is the report about their native country. Although it may seem to some teachers to be just "another assignment," it is more than that. It is purposeful. For academic reasons, children need to know how to report, search for information, organize material, read, summarize, paraphrase, and write. For cultural reasons, children need to experience a sense of continuity through the re-telling of their histories and religion as well as their expressions in language, art, and music. For psychological reasons, children need to have a place like the film-strips to make statements about their feelings and beliefs. There is a Latin saying, *Quod non est dictum non est in mundum:* "What is not said or expressed is not in the world." Dung, the young Vietnamese girl whom I revisited in Chapter 3, also advised teachers to bring out what is hidden within. Let them "talk, not just about everyday conversations, but about their feelings," she said.

My own model was a wise teacher herself. As a 14-year-old many years ago emerging from the silent stage or perhaps just too shy to speak, I sat in her Greek mythology class and listened as she assigned us to present an oral report on a Greek myth. There was something about that assignment, combined with my shyness to speak, that rendered me powerless. I could not fulfill the assignment. But inspired by an idea that would free me to speak in public, I approached her privately and asked to say something about my country instead—

quite a distance away from the Greeks. Without hesitation, she agreed enthusiastically. So I spoke about the Philippines. None of my peers objected, and the 15- to 20-minute oral presentation lasted an hour as the students asked questions about a topic that was familiar to me but unfamiliar to them. I held this teacher in great respect for the remainder of my school days.

I know from experience that the reports act as a vehicle for the children to express themselves and to reveal themselves to their new world. In class, the dialogues take care of their need for verbal communication about who they are and where they came from. The reports bring the verbal and written words together, and the children's old world emerges to become a part of their new history.

I give the children a list of things to include in the report. Throughout the year they are gathering information about their country, reading, interviewing their parents, sketching images, recording their music, tracing maps, and illustrating their flags, foods, and native dress. The list is not meant to be mere "foods and folktale" but a starting point for the children to research their histories, to document memories, and to be authentic. It is also meant for them not only to take pride in who they are, but to share with others their unique cultures' contributions to society. This information they place in a folder to be put together at the end of the year. I work with them at each step of the process, and the room is transformed into a workshop. When their books are completed, they make oral presentations in groups or individually. Once this is done, they plan the cultural ritual and celebration that completes the work of the year.

Report Procedures

During the first month of the year, much of the work of building cultural continuity is done orally. Where children are still breaking out of the silent stage, they speak to us through a friend. It is during this month that the children are taught to listen to one another attentively and to appreciate their differences. They bring things to share and I encourage them to bring or to wear their native clothing. Then they dance their dances and teach one another how to dance. I know from experience about the importance of dance, how it is not only a form of communication but an essential part of culture, as those of us partly schooled abroad have dances embedded inside us. As I watch the children, it is fascinating to see a boy from Samoa share his dance movements with children from Vietnam and then attempt to dance to music from India. At times when the children from Mexico dance to their lively music, everyone joins in. In the beginning, the girls participate in the dance easily; then, with some encouragement, the boys join in. If I find that the boys from Afghanistan are shy, then with the help of my bilingual assistant I bring in the elders and the men take the boys aside and teach them to dance.

During the second month of the year, the children's art sketches begin to take shape. They illustrate their artifacts, their flags, religious symbols, their former classrooms, alphabet forms, their native dress, and their foods. These non-verbal expressions and symbols of their cultures do touch something deeper in the children, because very often the room is quiet when they are drawing. (See pages 178–180.)

There are those who write something under their illustrations, and that is fine. The children know how much they wish to share. Once a child from Afghanistan wrote:

> *These are the clothes we wear in my country. In America we*
> *wear them at home, but we cannot wear them at school.*

I realized that here in the mind of the child was the beginning of a cultural split. So I looked for the opportunity for the class to share their histories and for the children to wear their native dress. If I stretched the time for them to sit in their "office desks" and do school-work, they would be comfortable in school wearing native dress if they wished. As a result of this experience, later in the year many of the children began to feel a closer connection between home and school and even felt comfortable wearing their native clothes to school without feeling that anyone would laugh at them. The other children then accepted it as natural. Thus, the threefold intervention came together.

Some of the unschooled or partially schooled children are still developing motor coordination and have difficulty tracing a map, using a pair of scissors, or even printing legibly. I work with them, and other children take turns assisting them. They have on their desks a list of peers who are responsible for them every hour while I am occupied, or they work with a bilingual assistant who gives us a couple of hours each day. These children, too, make a simple report.

During the third month, the children begin to read simple books about their country in any language and they then transfer the infor-mation into English with the help of translators. Many can do so themselves. During this month, they search the libraries for readable books. They interview their parents and members of their extended family. The children begin to write simple paragraphs, and I begin teaching them to paraphrase from books. This process takes time and may go on for many months. As children write their drafts, they practice their cursive writing or printing for excellence. I find that there is so much inside these children that they become involved and absorbed in their work—because it is meaningful to them.

Children in their Native Dress

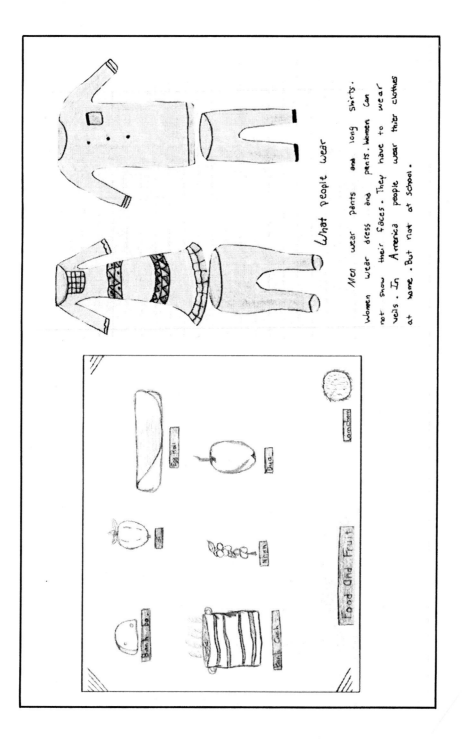

What People wear

Men wear pants and long shirts. Women wear dress and pants. Women can not show their faces. They have to wear veils. In America people wear their clothes at home. But not at School.

Food and Fruit

1.

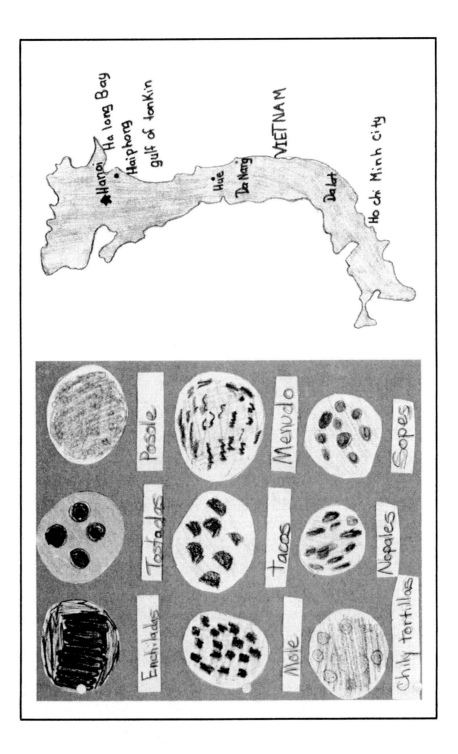

180

During the fourth month the children continue to read and research. By this time their reading skills are stronger; most are now at
about the second grade level in English, while some are reading
around the third grade level. Toward the end of the month, the children
have a wider reading range of books, and can begin to write their first
drafts in more than one paragraph. They either have their peers proof-
read or ask members of their extended family to help if they can. After
they pass their work through a proofreader, I correct it individually
with them and give them some professional ideas as to how they may
improve their written work and enhance their artwork. I find that the
children are earnest about learning and appreciate feedback if it is
sensitively done and the teacher is honest with them about the quality
of their work. Sometimes when children turn in work that is carelessly
executed, I return it to them and show them what I expect. If I have
high expectations, they do meet the standards of excellence—and I
believe this builds their self-esteem.

During the fifth month, the children begin to document their
experiences and thoughts about their country. I find that those who
have been through war may at this time feel safe to write, share, and
draw what they have seen and/or heard, trusting the teacher to understand their painful experience.

During the sixth month, the children design the cover of their
report and make pockets on the inside to house their cassette tapes. I
give their work one final check and help them with finishing touches.
Then they take cassette tapes home and I lend them portable tape
recorders to tape their family histories. Their parents speak in the
native language; the children translate into English. They do all the
taping during this month, and the final tapes are placed in the pockets.

During the seventh month, the children finish up their reports,
re-write, touch up the artwork, and schedule an oral presentation to
the entire class before the cultural ritual and celebration. These presentations may go on to the eighth month, because at this time of year
the school also schedules school assemblies and field trips.

During the eighth month, the children complete their presenta-
tions to the class and we begin to prepare for the cultural ritual and
celebration that complete the work. The reports are now turned in
and placed on a special table for reading and listening to the tapes
contained in the cover.

During the ninth month, the children focus their energy on closing
the academic gaps. They read books written at the fourth—and a few
at the fifth—grade levels. They become more comfortable reading
American history and learn how to outline and write a composition
after their field trips. Accustomed now to presenting reports, they take
the newspaper and report on the news; they continue writing in their
journals. If time permits, they may write a class newspaper.

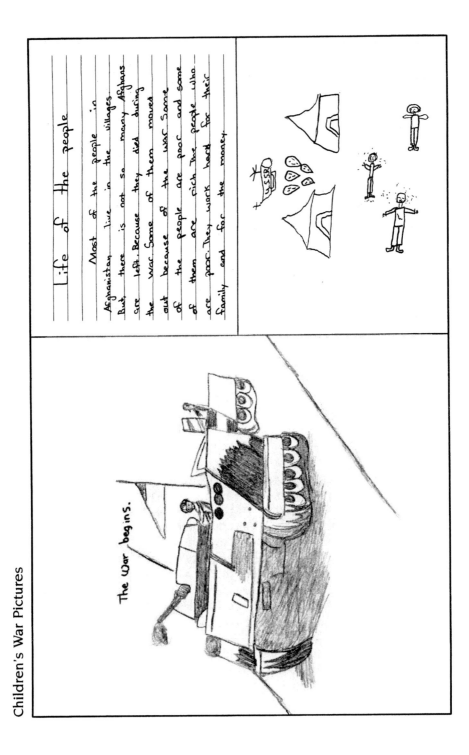

Life of the people

Most of the people in Afghanistan live in the villages. But, there is not so many Afghans are left. Because they died during the war. Some of them moved out because of the war. Some of the people are poor and some of them are rich. The people who are poor. They work hard for their family and for the money.

The War begins.

My thoughts about my country

When I want to write about my country, suddenly a lot of tears come to my eyes. Some of the tears drop off my eyes, because in Afghanistan I remember that there was a lot of fighting. One brother killed another brother. I was born in Kabul. I grew up in Afghanistan. I went to school. I learned a lot about my country, and I went to a city in Afghanistan called Ghazni. I have a lot of wishes for my country. I wish that there would be no more fighting, because I want to go back. I love my country. I love my people, the mountains, rivers, the skies and...

My thoughts about my country

My thoughts about my country is that I think that the weapon is stopped and I think weapon in my country and I wish that there will be no more war in my country

The Cultural Ritual

I think it is important for the children to make a statement of who they are. On this day, the children wear their native clothing if they have any and bring their artifacts to share. We sit in a circle and the children speak, read, or show excerpts from their reports. The children then share their music and dance their native dances. At the closing of the ritual ceremony, they partake in a variety of native dishes prepared by the parents, who stop by in the morning to bring the food.

Then the reports are placed on a special table, and during the week the children sign them out and read about each other's countries and cultures. Because the reports are designed with pockets for cassette tapes that contain their music, their language, and the children's translation into English, we set up a tape recorder with earphones so each person can listen to the tapes during the week and also read the reports. From the pages of their country reports, the children speak.

Giving Closure

I find that as the year comes to an end, it is important to begin giving closure together. The good-bye is very important so the children do not get depressed. One Afghan boy expressed his feelings one day: "Good-bye, little room, I am going to miss you."

Much of their life energy has been in the room. They have formed friendships, hung their best work all around the room, and shared their life histories. I try to teach the importance of good-byes as their next step of development. As each month passes I have seen their confidence build, so it is not a difficult closure but it needs to be done.

We spend some time talking about their future, what they have learned that they can take with them to the next grade or school, and what they can do during the summer months. They take down the bulletin boards carefully, respectfully; they gather their work into folders and prepare for their next adventure. I find that this is another time for a simple cultural celebration and dance, because music and dance always seem to soothe the soul.

Concluding Reflections

Throughout the pages of this book the children have expressed their thoughts and feelings about leaving their homeland and coming to the United States. The story begins with the silent Dennis and what

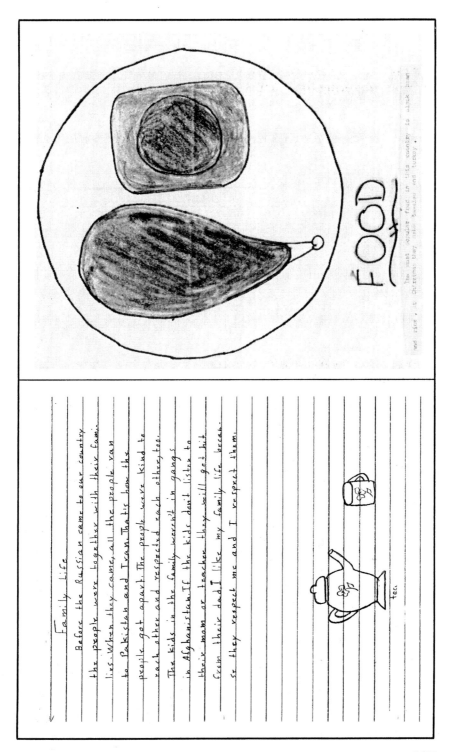

Family Life

Before the Russian came to our country the people were together with their families. When they came, all the people ran to Pakistan and Iran. That is how the people got apart. The people were kind to each other and respected each other too.

The kids in the family weren't in gangs in Afghanistan. If the kids don't listen to their mom or teacher they will get hit from their dad. I like my family life because they respect me and I respect them.

tea

FOOD

The most popular food in this country is chicken breast and rice. At Christmas they have tamales and turkey.

185

Dances

In Afghanistan there were lots of dances, but one good dance that people liked was Attan. They use this dance in marriage, weddings, and in the parties. This dance was for women and men. In the dance they need fifteen or twenty people.

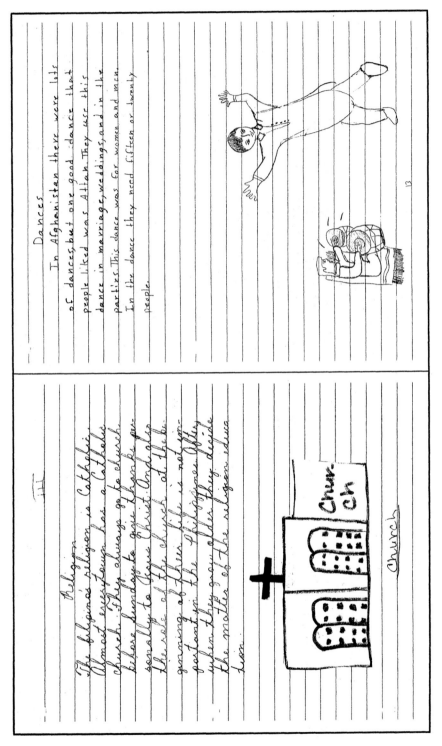

13

Religion

The Filipinos religion is Catholic. Almost everyone has a Catholic church. They always go to church before Sundays to give thanks personally to have Christ. And also the role of the church at the gaining of their life is very important in the Philippines. After when they grow older they decide the matter of the religion education.

Church

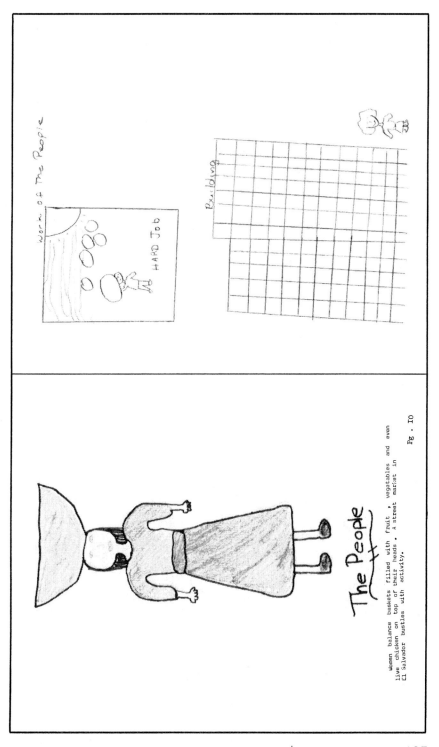

Work of The People

HARD Job

Reading

The People

Women balance baskets filled with fruit, vegetables and even live chicken on top of their heads. A street market in El Salvador bustles with activity.

Pg . IO

The dong ganh.

Work of the people

The work of Afghanistan is different. Some of them is hard and some of them is easy. The hard on are building house. The easy one is teachings. There is not mad work in Afghanistan. Some people are so poor that they knock on people door and beg for food or any thing. Some people are not working because they don't have working a lot. That they get 30 dollars for an whole day.

City life , Country life

In Afghanistan the people who live in the city are rich. The people who live in the village are not rich but,their not poor. In the cities they have buildings and in the country they have houses and apartments. In the city it is a very ok place and in the country it is a beautiful place. The country has lots of exciting things to see, Like for example the parks it has trees that are different colors. And the sea it's beautiful specialy when it is evening.

city

country

Alphabets.

Vietnam alphabet is a little bit different than the America alphabet.

Vietnam alphabet, some letters have 3 different and two different kinds, like A Ä Â. Some Vietnamese people the been in America for a year or more, Some of the forgot the alphabets Here is the Vietnam alphabet on the bottom.

A Ä Â B C D D Ê F G H
I K L M N O Ô Ơ P Q R S T U Ư
V X Y

it took to help him open the door to his silent world. He became alive when the cultural, academic, and psychological aspects of himself came together in the classroom. He made it into college with an integrated sense of self. Alice, Cindy, and Dung shared their inner worlds with us. Successful in academics, they went to college but their cultural selves were left behind. They awakened to their cultural split during our dialogues. Their plan for the future now, as young adults, includes the integration of their two worlds. Rosario shared her inner world with us, and although she made friends at last, she was unable to complete her senior year and was unable to go to college to join her friends.

As I began to give closure to this book, I located these five children again, now adults. Dennis is still "alive," active and working. Alice has successfully completed her college degree and is working. Her cultural self is more integrated. Cindy successfully completed her college degree and still sits "on the fence"—feeling that she belongs to neither the Chinese nor the American community. Dung is now married and working to complete her degree. Her cultural self is finally integrated. She is at home with herself. Rosario remains silent about the school experience and her desire to go to college. Her life is filled with work and relationships of family, friends, and child.

For these children, the traumatic uprooting experience included the pain of discrimination and the fears encountered in school. What they had to say is summarized here:

> *I come from another land, another culture. I have been un-earthed and am a seedling in a new land. The change upsets the kind of life I had. It is hard to go into a classroom.*

> *I feel as if everyone is looking at me and staring at me. I want to stay close to my family. I am afraid to leave them, but I must go to school.*

> *In my silence I have hopes and wishes. I wish that everything will turn out all right someday for I am not sure I am going to make it.*

Their message to the teacher guided me during my second experience with immigrant children to keep the dialogues alive. As they revealed their inner worlds, together we set the nest and created the environment for the true selves to emerge.

After a year of CAP intervention, what the second group of children had to say is summarized here:

> *I was very happy because we learned lots of things. We had art and reading and free play for 20 minutes.*
>
> GIRL FROM AFGHANISTAN

Yesterday's homework was fun because I had a test about who reads and understands better. I won my dad. It was great!

GIRL FROM EGYPT

Today, when I came to school, I was so happy. I like school because I can learn a lot of things.

GIRL FROM AFGHANISTAN

At home, I act the same way as I act in school.

BOY FROM AFGHANISTAN

I couldn't be happier.

GIRL FROM EGYPT

I shall close with a book written by the children.

The Class Book

My editor at St. Martin's Press, Naomi Silverman, stopped by for a visit one day and together we and the children all shared our stories. One spontaneous little girl from Afghanistan gave Naomi a rose. After asking questions about how a book is made, the children asked her to help them write their own book. She was delighted to become the children's editor as well. The next day we began the Class Book. It was a collaborative activity whereby we all sat and wrote the story together. Each cultural group of children told of the life they had in their countries and what life was like for them. We faxed the pages to "our" editor and she edited the text.

The children then illustrated the foods, the games they had played, and the school life they had experienced in their countries. They selected four class artists, Sam and Naseh Rahman, Phuc Nguyen, and Duy Vu, who collected everyone's ideas and put the drawings together. As my story ends, their story begins.

Friends Forever

Once we came to the United
States from all over the world.

We grew up in our own cultures.
It was fun being kids
in our countries.

We traveled here in so many
ways... on camels, cars, trains,
ships and airplanes.

game

going to school

food

In Afghanistan, we had
a good country life.

In Vietnam, we had a
difficult farm life.

In the Philippines, we had
a warm tropical life.

In Fiji, we had a good island life.

In Mexico, we had a good
country life.

In El Salvador, we had a
good tropical life.

In Romania, we had a
good town life.

Now we all learn together
in Room 9 -- a special place
like a second home.

We are kind to each other.
If you visit us, you'll
have friends forever.

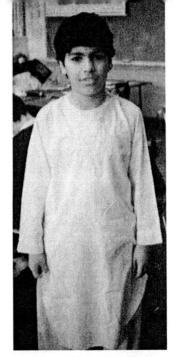

Suggested Readings

Ada, Alma Flor (1988a). Family interactions seen risked in language shift. *Education Week*. October 5, 1988.

Ada, A. F. (1988b). The Pajaro Valley experience: Working with Spanish-speaking parents to develop children's reading and writing skills in the home through the use of children's literature. In T. Skutnabb-Kangas & J. Cummins (Eds.), *Minority education: From shame to struggle* (pp. 223–238). Philadelphia: Multilingual Matters.

Ada, A. F. & Beutel C. (1991). "Participatory research as dialogue for action." Unpublished manuscript, University of San Francisco.

Aranowitz, M. (1985). The social and emotional adjustment of immigrant children: A review of the literature. *International Migration Review, 18*, 237–257.

Ashton-Warner, S. (1969). *Teacher.* New York: Simon & Schuster.

Au, K. H. & Jordan, C. (1981). Teaching reading to Hawaiian children: Finding a culturally appropriate solution. In H. Trueba, G. P. Guthrie & K. H. Au (Eds.), *Culture and the bilingual classroom: Studies in classroom ethnography.* (pp. 139–152). Rowley, MA: Newbury House.

Auerbach, E. (1990). *Making meaning, making change.* Boston: University of Massachusetts.

Auerbach, E. & Wallerstein, N. (1987). *English for the workplace: ESL in action, problem posing at work.* New York: Addison Wesley.

Bhatnager, J. (1980). Linguistic behaviour and adjustment of immigrant children in French and English schools in Montreal. *International Review of Applied Psychology. 29,* 141–149.

Bhatnager, J. (1981). Multiculturalism and education of immigrants in Canada. In J. Bhatnager (Ed.), *Educating immigrants* (pp. 69–95). New York: St. Martin's Press.

Bhatnager, J. (1981). *Educating immigrants.* New York: St. Martin's Press.

——— (1985). Language maintenance programs for immigrant children. *International Review of Applied Psychology, 34,* 503–526.

Campos, S. J. & Keatinge, H. R. (1988). The Carpinteria language minority student experience: From theory, to practice, to success. In T. Skutnabb-

Kangas & J. Cummins (Eds.), *Minority education: From shame to struggle* (pp. 299–307). Clevedon, England: Multilingual Matters.

Chall, J. S., & Snow, C. (1982). *Families and literacy: The contributions of out of school experiences to children's acquisition of literacy: A final report to the National Institute of Education.* Cambridge, MA: Harvard Families and Literacy Project.

Charlot, M. (1981). The education of immigrant children in France. In J. Bhatnager (Ed.), *Educating immigrants* (pp. 96–112). New York: St. Martin's Press.

Cummins, J. (1981). The role of primary language development in promoting educational success for language minority students. In *Schools and Language Minority Students: A theoretical framework.* Los Angeles: California State University.

Cummins, J. (1986). Empowering minority students: A framework for intervention. *Harvard Education Review, 56*, 18–36.

Daly, S. & Carpenter, J. (1985). Adjustment of Vietnamese refugee youths: A self-report. *Psychological Reports, 56*, 971–976.

Dawson, J. P. (1979). The intersection of Paulo Freire and C. G. Jung: A paradigm for education (Doctoral dissertation, Columbia University, 1979). *University Microfilm No. 80 06 798.* (Microfilm International, 300 N. Zeeb Road, Ann Arbor, MI 48106).

Dulay, H., & Burt, M. (1977). Remarks on creativity in second language acquisition. In M. Burt, H. Dulay & M. Finnocchiaro (Eds.), *Viewpoints on English as a second language.* New York: Regents, pp. 95–126.

Elley, W. 1984. Exploring the reading difficulties of second language learners in Fiji. In J. C. Alderson & A. Urquart (Eds.), *Reading in a second language.* New York: Longman, pp. 281–301.

Freire, P. (1973). *Education for critical consciousness.* New York: Seabury Press.

Freire, P. (1993). *Pedagogy of the oppressed.* New York: Continuum Press.

Fris, A. M. (1982). Policies for minority education. A comparative study of Britain and Sweden. Unpublished doctoral dissertation, University of Stockholm, Sweden.

Guiora, A. Z., Lane, H. L., & Bosworth, L. A. (1977). An exploration of some personality variables in authentic pronunciation of a second language. In H. L. Lane and E. M. Zale (Eds.), *Studies in Language and Language Behavior, 4*, 261–266.

Hirsch, E. D. (1987). *Cultural literacy: What every American needs to know.* Boston: Houghton Mifflin.

Kelley, G. P. (1981). Contemporary American policies and practices in the education of immigrant children. In J. Bhatnager (Ed.), *Educating immigrants.* New York: St. Martin's Press.

Krashen, S. & Terrell, D. (1983). *The Natural Approach: Language Acquisition in the Classroom.* Hayward, CA: Alemany Press.

Liu, W. T., Lamana, M., & Muratta, A. (1979). *Transition to nowhere: Vietnamese refugees in America.* Nashville, TN: Charter House.

Maguire, Patricia (1987). *Doing participatory research: A feminist approach.* Amherst, MA: The Center for International Education, School of Education, University of Massachusetts.

McCaleb, Sudia Paloma. (1994). *Building communities of learners: A collaboration among teachers, students, families, and community.* New York: St. Martin's Press.

Nieto, S. (1992). *Affirming diversity: The socio-political context of multicultural education.* New York: Longman Publishing Group.

Patron, Rose Lee (1988). *Promoting English literacy for Spanish-speaking students: A participatory study of Spanish-speaking parents, their children and school personnel, using an innovative intervention model in Spanish.* Unpublished doctoral dissertation presented to the faculty of the School of Education, Multicultural Education Program, University of San Francisco.

Reichmuth, Stella (1988). *Hispanic parent empowerment through critical dialogue and parent-child interaction within the school setting.* Unpublished doctoral dissertation presented to the faculty of the School of Education, Multicultural Education Program, University of San Francisco.

Reyes, M. (1992, Winter). Challenge venerable assumptions: Literacy instruction for linguistically different students. *Harvard Educational Review, 62* (1), 427–438.

Skutnabb-Kangas, Tove (1981). *Bilingualism or not: The education of minorities.* Clevedon, England: Multilingual Matters.

Snow, C., Barnes, W., Chandler, J., Goodman, I., & Hemphill, H. (1991). *Unfulfilled expectations: Home and school influences on literacy.* Cambridge, MA: Harvard University Press.

Spring, J. (1994). *Deculturalization and the struggle for equality: A brief history of the education of dominated cultures in the United States.* New York: McGraw-Hill.

Terrell, Tracy D. (November 1977). "A Natural Approach to Second Language Acquisition and Learning." *Modern Language Journal,* LXI (7), 325–337.

Torres-Guzman, M. E., & Perez, B. (1992). *Learning in two worlds: An integrated Spanish/English biliteracy approach.* White Plains, NY: Longman Publishing Group.

Trueba, Henry T. (1984). The forms, functions and values of literacy: Reading for survival in a barrio as a student. *NABE Journal,* Vol. IX (1), 21–39.

Wong-Fillmore, L. (1983). The language learner as an individual: Implications of research on individual differences for the ESL teacher. In M. A. Clarke & J. Handscombe (Eds.), *On TESOL '82; Pacific perspectives on language learning and teaching* (pp. 157–171). Washington, D.C.: TESOL.

References

Ada, A. F. (1993). *Mother-tongue, literacy as a bridge between home and school cultures: The power of two languages*. New York: McGraw-Hill School Publishing.

Barker, J. (1993). Personal communication.

Beutel, C. (1993). Personal communication.

Bhatnager, J. (1981). Multiculturalism and education of immigrants in Canada. In J. Bhatnager (Ed.), *Educating immigrants* (pp. 69–95). New York: St. Martin's Press.

Bowers, C. A. (1984). *The promise of theory: Education and the politics of cultural change*. New York: Longman, Green.

Chao, R., & Sung, B. L. (1977). *Chinese immigrant children* (Preliminary Report Monograph No. 5). New York: City University, Department of Asian Studies. (ERIC Document Reproduction Service No. ED 152 895)

Cummins, J. (1986). Empowering minority students: A framework for intervention. *Harvard Education Review, 56,* 18–36.

de Castillejo, I. C. (1974). *Knowing Woman. A Feminine Psychology*. New York: Harper Colophon Books, Harper & Row.

Diccionario manual e ilustrado de la lengua Española (2nd ed.). Madrid: Espasa-Calpe, S.A. (Original work published 1950)

Freire, P. (1984). *Pedagogy of the oppressed*. New York: Continuum Press.

Gadamer, H. G. (1976). *Philosophical Hermeneutics*. Berkeley: University of California Press.

Grossenbacher, F. (1988). Personal communication.

Hart, T. (1993). Personal communication.

Henderson, J. L. (1984). *Cultural attitudes in psychological perspective*. Toronto, Canada: Inner City Books.

Igoa, C. (1988). *Toward a psychology and education of the uprooted: A study of the inner world of immigrant children*. Doctoral dissertation, University of San Francisco.

Kelley, G. P. (1981). Contemporary American policies and practices in the education of immigrant children. In J. Bhatnager (Ed.), *Educating immigrants*. New York: St. Martin's Press.

Kieffer, C. (1981). *Doing dialogic retrospection: Approaching empowerment through participatory research*. Paper presented at the International Meeting of the Society for Applied Anthropology, University of Edinburgh, Scotland.

Liljestrom, R., Noren-Bjorn, E., Schyl-Bjurman, G., Ohrn, B., Gustafsson, L. H. & Lofgren, O. (1982). *Young Children in China*. Translated by Tove Skutnabb-Kangas and Robert Phillipson. Clevedon, Avon BS217HH, England: Multilinguan Matters Ltd.

Milner, D. (1983). *Children and Race*. Harmondsworth, England: Penguin.

Oberg, K. (1960). Culture shock: Adjustment to new cultural environments. *Practical Anthropology, 7*, 177–182.

Raoufi, S. (1981). The children of guest-workers in the Federal Republic of Germany: Maladjustment and its effects on academic performance. In J. Bhatnager (Ed.), *Educating Immigrants*. New York: St. Martin's Press.

Schramm, W., Nelson, L. M., & Bethan, M. T. (1981). *Bold Experiment. The Story of Educational Television in American Samoa*. Stanford, CA: Stanford University Press.

Smalley, W. A. (1963). Culture shock, language shock and the shock of self-discovery. *Practical Anthropology, 10*, 45–56.

Smith, F. (1992, February). Learning to read: The never-ending debate. *Phi Delta Kappan, 434.*

Sokoloff, B., Carlin, J., & Pham, H. (1984). Five-year follow-up of Vietnamese refugee children in the United States. *Clinical Pediatrics, 23* 10:565–570. Los Angeles, CA.

Spring, J. (1994). *Deculturalization and the struggle for equality: A brief history of the education of dominated cultures in the United States*. New York: McGraw-Hill.

Trueba, H. T. (1993). Lessons learned: The healing of American society. In H. T. Trueba, C. Rodriguez, Y. Zou, & J. Cintrón, *Healing multicultural America* (pp. 133–154). Washington, DC: Falmer Press.

Von Franz, M. L. (1970). *An introduction to the interpretation of fairy tales*. New York: Spring Publications.

Wickes, F. G. (1966). *The inner world of childhood* (rev. ed.). New York: Appleton-Century. (Original work published 1955)

———. (1988). *The inner world of childhood* (rev. ed.). Boston: Sigo Press.

Wilson, G. (1986). Personal communication.

———. (1987). Personal communication.

———. (1988). Personal communication.

Index